YOUTH ALPHA
LEADERS' GUIDE

ISBN 978-1-904074-32-8

Published by Alpha International
Holy Trinity Brompton
Brompton Road, London, SW7 1JA

Email: publications@alpha.org

Contents

Thanks

This manual is the result of much hard work, only a fraction of it mine. There have been lots of people who have been running Youth Alpha around the world and who have contributed the fruits of their experience in illustrations, games and video clips suggestions. I would also like to thank those who have written articles for this manual.

Thanks, lastly, to my employers, the South American Mission Society, who, with a true spirit of cooperation in mission, allowed me time out to work on this project.

Jonathan Brant

SECTION I
INTRODUCTION

Introduction to Youth Alpha

This manual is an Alpha publication.

The Alpha course is a practical introduction to the Christian faith developed by Holy Trinity Brompton in London. The course has been extraordinarily successful at bringing people to faith and enthusing existing Christians. Today there are over 33,500 courses running around the world and more than 10 million people have taken part.

The remarkable story of the Alpha course, especially its appeal to young adults, has encouraged many people to run an adapted course for young people. These courses have also taken place around the world and seen success, but the challenge continues to be great – there is a desperate need within the church to reach and keep young people. In the UK for example, it is estimated that by the age of sixteen 98 per cent of young people who once attended church no longer do so. And statistics suggest that only 7 per cent of those under 18 years of age have any regular contact with 'organised religion'.

These resources are an update of previous Youth Alpha materials. They are an attempt to keep fresh and creative and to give you the best possible chance of using Alpha to reach young people with the good news of Jesus Christ.

We hope that this manual will equip you to bring alive the truth of God's love to those who have grown tired of listening AND to those who have never heard.

Stories from the frontlines

Youth Alpha has already been in action across the world, from Australia to Sweden and from Iceland to the Seychelles. It has been used by big churches with flourishing youth ministries, and by individuals whose passion for young people prompts them to open their homes and invite youth in. Here are three brief stories of Youth Alpha running in different places and in different ways. I hope that they will encourage you, and help you to picture what a Youth Alpha course might look like in your particular situation.

Story 1

G'DAY! I'm P-J Taylor from Adelaide in South Australia and I'm the Youth Pastor at Rosefield Uniting Church. Youth Alpha has really impacted the young people here. Our first two courses were run at . . . believe it or not . . . my place! We had about 10 youth come along on a Tuesday night at 5:30pm. We used the lounge/dining area, and as young people arrived they were greeted by music, video clips, snacks and drinks – and the smell of dinner on the way. We began with dinner all together for the first half-hour, which was a real hit. Some would come back each week just wanting to know 'What's for tea?'! I did the cooking before they came and basically made simple but yummy meals, such as super hot dogs, hamburgers, pasta, tacos, hot potatoes, fish fingers and fries etc.

Then we got into the sessions, which went for about 30–40 minutes all up, including music/activities/games/illustrations/get-to-know-you bits/video clips etc. I play guitar, so about half way through the course we began singing some choruses to begin the sessions instead of having ice-breakers and the like.

There were two of us doing the talks in the sessions each week, taking it in turns making the various points. If there were three points, for example, I might do point one and three and the other leader would do point two. This gave the youth some diversity in the presentation. Both of us also took a small group after the talks. We had a guys' group and a girls' group. This worked really well for the high school age group as more honest discussion was able to flow without the 'distractions'. Small groups were definitely a highlight. It is amazing hearing the first prayers that youth say out loud, or hearing the deep thoughts and opinions that come out from teenagers' minds.

The night usually ended with dessert – the food always seemed to be a hit for some reason! The camp too was fantastic, held at a holiday home on the beach. The Holy Spirit stuff was well received and it certainly changed some lives.

Some comments we received at the end of the course include:

- 'I have found true meaning for my life.'
- 'I feel closer to God and happier in a way.'
- 'I was filled with the Holy Spirit – I am a real Christian now!'
- 'My faith is stronger.'
- 'Youth Alpha was the best thing in my life!'

Now we're running it in the church's youth room and past Youth Alpha students have become helpers and small group leaders. It's very rewarding seeing past participants getting up and helping present one of the points in a talk, or encouraging their peers in the small groups, or helping in the kitchen.

It certainly works well in a small setting and it can be a lot of fun getting to know one another over that time.

P-J Taylor
Youth Pastor, Rosefield Uniting Church
Regional Youth Alpha Adviser, South Australia

Story 2

The first time I was involved in running Youth Alpha in a parish context, we ran it alongside an adult Alpha course. Sometimes we shared food, adults and young people together; at other times the young people ate pizza and the like a little less formally, but there remained a sense of family, each group conscious of the presence of the other. Our team met weekly to prepare each session. With the resource of ideas from the Leaders' Manual, we used our own gifts and creativity to facilitate a session that was welcoming and provided room for the young people to discuss and ask questions. We used ice-breakers; we watched video clips and sometimes we invited in speakers; young leaders facilitated small groups; we had times of prayer and used new worship music to help us.

The experience of belonging to a group was appreciated by the young people and they became very supportive of one another. This was an opportunity for young Catholics to invite their friends to come along to something other than Mass. We need such opportunities.

Mary Hughes
Hexham and Newcastle Diocesan Youth Mission Team

Story 3

The Path is a youth congregation of about 250 young people based at Trinity Church, Cheltenham in the south-west of England. It was first established in 1996 and involves young people from over 30 different church-based youth groups from across the region. These groups meet together for main celebrations, incorporating worship, teaching and prayer ministry in an authentic and yet relevant fashion, on a fortnightly basis. The congregation exists to model church for young people and to equip them to be the difference in their own communities. To this effect the Path reaches out to different areas of the youth community through a variety of programmes and initiatives to encourage young people to play their part in God's Great Commission.

Central to the mission of the Path is the small group. Small groups form the vital structure and foundation from which all activities are based – they provide a place of belonging and a place from which to serve. Getting young people into a small group culture is not so difficult; involving people in the right small group is more of a challenge. One way in which this challenge has been pursued has been through the Alpha programme. The Path has been running Youth Alpha courses for three years and is now directly connected with seven schools across the region and indirectly linked with many more, as young leaders take the vision and values of Youth Alpha from the Path into their own communities.

All of the leadership undertake regular in-house training to prepare and equip for the Youth Alpha programmes, which have so far reached out to several hundred young people. Youth Alpha courses in schools differ from those that are run during the evenings for the youth at church. Attempts have also been pursued to take Youth Alpha into the café-bar culture in the town.

One of the most significant parts of the Youth Alpha programme is typically referred to as the 'Holy Spirit Weekend'. The Path uses the opportunity presented by half term holidays to take Alpha participants from all current programmes and to bring them together for a long weekend houseparty to provide a place of safety, a place free from distraction, a place to belong, and a place from which to discover.

The Path celebrated its sixth anniversary by taking over 90 young people away on such a houseparty, after which a number of young believers returned home and were baptised as an outward expression of their faith and the difference that God had made in their lives as a consequence of completing the Youth Alpha course.

These Youth Alpha 'graduates' are then placed into small groups where they can explore their faith in greater depth and develop the principles of discipleship. As Youth Alpha is an ongoing initiative, every young person, no matter how young or old in their faith, is encouraged to invite friends to subsequent courses. Frequent social events and parties are held to provide opportunities for interaction and invitation to the next course, and many of the graduates are themselves invited to take part once again in future courses as a 'helper'; indeed some Youth Alpha graduates are now themselves leading Youth Alpha discussions.

As for the Path, Youth Alpha is by no means the only entry point, but over the past three years it has developed into our largest 'front door'. We incorporate multimedia where appropriate and modify programmes where time necessitates. At the end of the programme one thing remains constant: we see lives changed and young people seeking the Lord, living life to the full for Jesus, and eager to play their part in God's Great Commission.

Scott Andrews
Senior Pastor
The Path – Equipping Young People 2 B the Difference

How to use this manual

The first thing to say is that this manual is a reference tool, a resource. Don't feel that you have to read it from cover to cover, all at once. One goal has been to take the relative newcomer to youth ministry through a step-by-step process of strategising, planning, preparing and presenting the material. For those of you with more experience this might mean that certain sections of the manual seem too basic. Please don't feel you have to plough through pages of what you already know, or struggle over ground you have already covered – just jump to the sections that are relevant.

The manual is divided into six sections. These are the objectives of each section:

1. Introduction	You're practically through this one
2. Strategy	What kind of course will you run?
3. Planning and Preparing	The crucial months leading up to a course
4. Practical Skills	To help equip you with some essential leadership skills
5. The Three Streams	The 15 sessions of Alpha presented in three streams
6. Appendices	Forms, flyers and other bits and pieces for your use.

The adult Alpha course has been effective in a wide range of contexts and churches. This integration of Alpha into the world church means that those who have been inspired by the adult course, and are now looking to run Youth Alpha, come from a great diversity of situations. The structure and content of this manual is driven by a desire to help as many of those people as possible 'build' a Youth Alpha course that is appropriate for the young people they are reaching out to.

One innovation has been to present each of the 15 Alpha sessions in three different ways. These are the three streams named: Alpha-Tech, Alpha-Active and Alpha-Lite; their different flavours, target groups and goals will be explained later. Once again the desire is to make the material applicable in as wide a range of situations as possible and the streams are not intended to limit you but to resource you. For this reason each stream follows a very similar structure so that you can mix and match segments from the different streams to build the session that is as close as possible to being perfect for the needs of your group.

It is important to realise from the start that Youth Alpha is not a course in its own right, and these materials are not independent in content or structure. This manual is a tool to help adapt the Alpha course and the Alpha material for use with young people. There are those that argue that a 15 session systematic course is simply not a useful method of introducing today's young people to the Christian faith. Their arguments are not without merit. However, there is another side.

Many youth specialists believe that the pendulum has swung too far towards materials and programmes that are topical and issue based, sessions focused on relationships, the environment, sexuality or self-worth. As a result youth workers see many young people who have an idea of what Christianity might have to say to specific areas of their lives, but no real concept of what Christianity itself is. Alpha, with its broad foundational content, is perfectly suited to redress this balance both in mission to the unchurched and in discipling Christian youth. In any case Youth Alpha is not just about 'teaching'. Alpha is an invitation into community, into new experiences and into real and open discussion about issues of faith. Youth Alpha will only be truly effective in the hands of a leader who is committed to the structure and content of Alpha.

This guide is not intended to tell you what to do, or to be an official blueprint. It is intended as a resource to help you and encourage you. It is not intended to stifle your ideas or clamp down on your creativity. The work that it has done for you should free up time (that might otherwise be used working on session outlines or putting together worksheets) for you to focus on your young people, thinking, praying and acting to make the course as relevant, exciting and powerful as possible.

Don't feel constrained by this manual; feel liberated.

SECTION II
STRATEGY

Is Youth Alpha for me and my church?

There are few things more embarrassing than arriving at the check-out with a huge trolley load of shopping, which has already been selected, taken off the shelves, loaded on to the trolley, unloaded off the trolley, passed down the conveyor belt, scanned and packed into bags, and then finding that you don't have your wallet with you, or more embarrassing still that you have your wallet but no cash, or you have your credit card but no credit!

At least a trolley-load of shopping can be put back, or, if you've really lost it you can quietly walk away from it all and know that nothing is damaged apart from your pride and the check-out clerk's afternoon. To be halfway into a Youth Alpha course and then find that you don't have the resources - financial, human, emotional, or spiritual - to continue could have far more serious consequences.

There is a tendency for the hard-pressed youth worker, the volunteer with a family and a full time job, or the pastor with nobody under 65 in his or her church to hear the testimonies about a course like Alpha and think, 'This could be it!' In a way they are right: this could turn things around, bring young people into your church and, more importantly, introduce them to Jesus. But Youth Alpha is only a tool.

If Youth Alpha is to be effective in your church or your situation then it must fit into a wider strategy and vision that you have for work with young people. You must have a good idea of where the young people who will do the course will come from. They won't fall from heaven, and they are unlikely to wander in off the streets; they have better things to do with their time (or 'other' things at least). There must be a genuine desire in the church at large to welcome new young people into the fellowship in spite of the potential for friction that they bring. You must also have an initial plan for how they will be cared for and discipled when the course is over.

As you read through this section on strategy we hope that we can suggest ways for you to move forward. If you are not ready to run Youth Alpha this term there is always next term or next year.

Consider this self-assessment before you move on

1. Are we prepared to commit ourselves to young people before, during and after the course has finished?

2. Have we considered the implications (eg on time, family, social life, the church) of taking on and running Youth Alpha?

3. How do we plan to accommodate those young people who become Christians during the course?

   What about those who have not yet decided to follow Christ but are still seriously interested?

   What about those who attended the course but appeared to show no interest at all?

4. To what extent are parents, leaders and the local church behind Youth Alpha?

5. Who is praying for us and for the young people involved?

6. To what extent is the local church prepared to change and adapt as a result of the Youth Alpha course?

What makes a good Youth Alpha leader?

There is a well-worn cliché which states that 'Christianity is caught, not taught'. Youth Alpha represents a wonderful opportunity to model the Christian life to young people. A young person is much more likely to opt for the Youth Alpha course on the basis of their relationship with the leaders than because of the content of the course itself. Our whole approach and attitude must show that we are committed to them (Philippians 2:5–8). One of the keys to running a successful Youth Alpha Course is selecting and envisioning the team. There is much more about this in the Planning and Preparing and Practical Skills sections, but for now it is worth saying that all that follows should apply to your team as well as to you as the overall leader.

Live alongside the young people

The word became flesh and lived among us (John 1:14). We need to 'live' among the young people. We must be prepared to go to their world and meet them on their terms. They would rather that you were honest and open with them than that you were a brilliant leader who ran spectacularly successful Youth Alpha sessions (though of course it is possible to be both).

Have a current relationship with Jesus

Young people may not read the Bible too often but when they spend time with you they will certainly 'read' your life (see 1 Thessalonians 2:8). You don't have to be a saint or perfect – in fact watching you deal with difficulties and weakness is good for the young people – but your relationship with Jesus needs to be alive and kicking if it is to impact them.

Know that it is people that count, not programmes

Find out as much as you can about the young people. What influences those you are in contact with? What was the last film they saw? What is their favourite music? What 'soaps' do they watch? What do they spend their money on? Young people need to know that you understand and relate to their lives and that you love and accept them unconditionally. They need to know that you are committed to spending time and

energy on them without also demanding that they respond to your message, change and grow. This is a freeing kind of love, which releases the young people from the tyranny of feeling that they have to please you.

Know that it's not just about results

Are you prepared to run a whole Youth Alpha course and see no 'results' at the end of it?
The young people are not just fodder for the Youth Alpha course. Do not run the course because you feel 'someone's got to' or because 'the church needs more young people'. The young people will soon pick up on it.

Helping young people grasp the good news of Christ through Youth Alpha is tremendously exciting. It is also a sacrifice. It will involve a commitment to pray as well as a lot of time and energy. Ask God to show you his love and concern for them.

A few hints . . .

Don't

- be quick to judge outward appearances or appear shocked by what they may tell you
- take a swing in mood or temperament personally
- expect them to believe or do something you would not be prepared to believe or do
- expect to get on brilliantly with every young person
- feel that every session or chat with a young person has to be what you call productive
- ever put them down or attack their self-respect.

Do

- pray for them
- get involved with them – 'walk in their shoes'
- be prepared to be vulnerable and open yourself
- be prepared to listen to them
- be prepared to be confidential and trustworthy
- affirm and encourage them whenever you can
- be aware that physical contact can be open to misunderstanding

- be yourself
- enjoy yourself!

Targeting your Youth Alpha course

If you have got this far and are still reading it should be

- because you have a sense of commitment to Youth Alpha that comes from a realistic idea of the demands it will place on you and your church and a sense that you have the necessary resources to meet those demands
- because you have a sense of 'what makes a good Youth Alpha leader' and believe that you or your team have what it takes.

Now is the time to think more seriously about what kind of Youth Alpha course you are going to run.

We will address this through a series of questions:

- What is the AIM of the course?
- WHO is the course for?
- WHERE will the course take place?
- WHEN will the course take place?
- WHICH stream will the course follow?

The timetable given in the 'Planning and Preparing' section of this manual suggests that you should be addressing these questions, at least in principle, some three to six months in advance of your proposed start date. Once you have answered these questions you should be ready to move on to the practicalities of planning and preparation with a clear picture in your mind of what the goals are for your course, who the course will appeal to, the ways in which the programme and teaching content (as well as venue and timing) are moulded around the target group and its needs, and what an actual session might look like.

What is the aim of the course?

To some this question might seem redundant. 'Alpha is an introduction to the Christian faith, isn't it?' or 'The aim is to see young people come to faith in Jesus Christ, of course.' Well that is true, but the Youth Alpha course is also used for other purposes.

Other possibilities include:

- as a tool for discipleship

- for renewing and deepening previous faith commitments
- for more systematic teaching about Christianity to Christian youth
- as part of a course to lead up to confirmation in the Anglican or Roman Catholic Church
- as a means of group building for young people already attending church.

Youth Alpha is primarily mission-focused – we want to see young people meet Jesus – but it is a good tool for any of the above purposes and you should not feel that you are misusing it if you choose to run it in some context other than out-and-out mission. However, it is important that you are clear from the outset about how you will be using the course and what your goals are. You will not normally be successful if you are trying to achieve more than one of these aims at once.

Who is the course for?

Any thought about the aim of the course leads almost immediately into questions about who the course is aimed at. Giving careful consideration to this question is probably the key stage in your strategising.

Let's start by assuming that you are intending to run the course for young people (Why else would you choose this manual?) and then outline the most likely groups you could be trying to reach.

Possibilities include:

- young people already actively involved in your church
- young people on the fringe (non-attending children of church members, siblings or friends of church youth)
- young people associated with a local club or organisation
- young people in a local school.

Young people already actively involved in your church

As explained in the previous section, it is not unusual to use Youth Alpha with young people already attending church.

You might wish to run the course as a means of bringing an as yet unrelated group of young people together with the goal that they will then continue on as some kind of church youth group.

You might wish to run the course as a means of teaching, discipleship or any of the other possibilities listed above.

Note: If it is your ultimate goal to use the course as mission then you need to start with mission, even if you only have one or two non-Christians attending. If you run the course for your own young people first, it will be hard to motivate them to invite friends in the future as they will see the course as just another teaching curriculum. (However, one or two excellent demo-sessions might give them confidence to bring their friends when the course itself starts.)

Young people with little connection to your church

If you are planning to use the course to reach out to teenagers you don't know so well you need to ask yourself:

Is there already a core group of young people within our church set-up?

This is not just a few younger people scattered across the youth age range, rather a living functioning group where there are already relationships, and an established habit of meeting together – be that in structured youth activities or simply socially. Size is unimportant: a Youth Alpha course does not have to be large to be successful. It is important that the guests feel welcome.

If there is such a group then you are probably ready to start with a course based around the core group that already exists. Start thinking carefully about the group that is already in existence. Who are they? What are their interests? Who are their friends? These friends will almost certainly be people you might want to invite. If you can instil in them a sense of ownership of the Youth Alpha course then there is every chance the course will be a good experience for everyone.

If there is not already a living, breathing core group then you might not be ready to reach out to the fringe. A time of drawing together the young people already present in the church might be the way forward.

Young people associated with a local club or organisation

Many churches are involved in running or helping with different kinds of youth clubs or organisations in their locality. These might include: sports clubs, Scouts or Guides, open/ drop-in youth centres, social work or training projects, choirs or drama societies. These gatherings of young people present an interesting and challenging mission field and running a Youth Alpha course that is principally aimed at these young people could see great success.

If it is to be successful it will be because you, your leaders or your churched young people already have strong relationships with the young people attending the club or organisation. Young people will not normally make the transition from a sports club (for example) to a Youth Alpha course just because it is offered to them. They might make the transition if they know that half of the team (the churched youth), or the coaches (your leaders) are going to be there.

Young people in a local school

Once again the success of Youth Alpha in a local school is all about relationship. If you have a good relationship with the school, and with the students attending it, then a Youth Alpha course could be very successful.

If you are interested in schools turn to the article in the 'Practical Skills' section on working in schools and also to the schools part of the 'Planning and Preparing' section (see pages 25–6, 57–8.)

By now you should have an idea of who might like to invite. Take some time to think about this group of young people:

- What are their ages?
- What is their current level of contact with the church?
- What are their main leisure interests?
- Which causes or issues animate them?
- What is their level of education?
- What is it that makes them a definable group?
- What clothing labels do they wear?
- What music do they listen to?
- What films do they watch?

- What responsibilities/time commitments do they have?

It is important that the course is tailored to the needs, values and lifestyles of the group. Findingout the answers to these questions can help you to understand the level of knowledge, intent and ability of the guests and make the course as interesting as possible.

Where will the course take place?

This might sound like a minor point to be addressed once everything else is in place, but in fact it goes right to the heart of the success of the course because it deals with the sense of well-being and comfort of the young people. It is a crucial decision because of its impact on questions such as:

- Will they come?
- Will they be able to get to the venue?
- Will they stay around or get bored?
- Will they be relaxed?

Most of the time it will not be good enough just to assume that because there is space available on the church premises this is the place to run Youth Alpha. Here are some options and some thoughts on who they might or might not suit.

The church – OK if you are targeting church young people, but might be an extra hurdle to be overcome for unchurched young people.
Community centre – intended to serve the community and therefore not too expensive to hire.
Sports hall – well worth considering with the younger age group who will benefit from the chance to play some energetic games, and with those who are seriously into sport.
Home – if your group's going to be small then a home will invite a sense of belonging and familiarity. The home of one of the participants might be less threatening than the leader's home.
Fast food restaurant – these tend to be home turf to young people and many of them have small side rooms (often used for kids' parties etc.) that they might be willing to let you use. (You will probably have to promise to consume a quantity of burgers and soft drinks!)
Youth club/café/non-alcoholic bar – perhaps the churches in your town, or a parachurch youth

organisation, have a drop-in centre that they won't mind you using. Perhaps Youth Alpha could be an excuse to get different youth ministries in your area working together.
The great outdoors – if you have the climate for it and you can guarantee some peace and quiet when it is needed, then why not?

When will the course take place?

Before settling on a day of the week or a time of the day you will need to do some serious research into the lives of your potential guests. Once again, just picking the time of your usual youth meeting (if you have one) might not be the best if you are hoping to appeal to new young people. The first rule of making this kind of decision is to realise that you may never find a time that is perfect for everybody. Try to exclude as few as possible by considering these questions:

- What are their hours of work or schooling?
- What transport will they be using to arrive at the course?
- When is it convenient to use this form of transport?
- What kind of evening/weekend commitments do they already have? (Clubs, jobs, sports teams, night to go out on the town, homework, family)
- What are their parents' attitudes to activities on weeknights?

Which stream is for us?

Each of the 15 Youth Alpha sessions are presented in three different streams in the second half of this guide: Alpha-Tech, Alpha-Active, and Alpha-Lite. Now that you have identified your guests, considered their unique needs, and thought a little about the time of your meetings, and the type of venue you will be using, it is worth making an initial assessment of which of the three streams is most likely to suit your requirements.

Once again, it is worth stating that this method of presentation is not intended to cramp you or suppress your creativity. It is of special importance that you don't allow the video clips, illustrations and visual aids offered here to take over from the team's personal stories and insights. Nothing impacts young people as much as personal testimony.

There is no obligation to follow one of the three streams in its entirety. It is possible that you will want to mix and match components of the different streams in each session that you run, or that part way through a course you might recognise that one of the other approaches would serve you better. To use some computer jargon, the streams have been designed in such a way as to make the different components 'hot-swappable' from one stream to another.

General information

Each stream is based on the material presented in *Alpha - Questions of Life* and covered on an adult Alpha course. The information given is intended to equip you to present this material to a group of young people as effectively as possible. You will probably find that more is provided than you can use in any given session. This is intended to allow you greater flexibility in your presentation.

Session categories

Introductory Session
- Is There More to Life than This?
- To be used at a special kick-off event or school assembly.

Sessions 1–10
- The main body of the course presented over 10 weeks.

Weekend Sessions 1–4
- Presented as part of a weekend or day away.
- Usually takes place as soon as possible after Session 6.

(Note: In the 'Alpha-Lite Stream' Sessions 1–10 are compressed into 1–8.)

Session structure

Each session in each stream includes these basic components:

Arrival: A fun and all-embracing 'opener' appropriate to the different streams.
Introduction to session: A welcome, and an insight into what is to come from a course leader.
Getting to know one another: This part of the session is the equivalent of the meal eaten sociably in small groups on the adult Alpha course.

Youth Alpha teaching material: The Alpha content presented in a manner appropriate to the different streams. Including:
    Introduction – an attention grabber and issue raiser
    Teaching points – covering the Alpha material
    Conclusion/Practical application – to ground the teaching in reality
Activity or discussion in small groups: A chance to reflect on and develop the relevant parts of the teaching material.

The Three Streams

The particular flavours and the different goals of the three streams are introduced here through brief descriptive paragraphs and a quick-reference table. Once you have taken in this overview it is suggested you skim through the general information and the sessions in each of the streams themselves, to get a better idea of how this works out in practice.

Stream 1 – Alpha-Tech

This stream is called 'tech' because it uses multimedia technology, and because it engages with the Alpha teaching material in a technical/cerebral way. The participants should be confident and willing to engage with abstract ideas and to discuss them in a manner similar to that used on the adult Alpha courses. This stream is best suited to older youth and those who have had some exposure to Christianity, perhaps through past contact with the church or through Religious Education in school.

Stream 2 – Alpha-Active

This stream is called 'active' because the young people involved interact with the Alpha teaching material primarily through activity. Active games open the sessions and visual aids, drama sketches and content-related tasks take the place of abstract talks and small group discussion. This stream is best suited to younger youth, and those who are not academically motivated or comfortable with book culture.

Stream 3 – Alpha-Lite

This stream is called 'lite' because it is shorter, because of the greatly reduced responsibility upon the leader (both in preparation and presentation), and because of the relaxed approach that it takes to the presentation of the Alpha teaching material. In this stream the emphasis is on exploring Christianity together, primarily through looking at some brief stories that illustrate some of the themes taught in the Alpha course. The leader does not have to stand up and make a presentation, but can simply guide the group through the material. This stream is suited to use in schools, particularly to small groups that are peer led, and to situations where a full-blown course is impossible due to time constraints or lack of experienced, confident leaders.

	Stream 1 'Alpha-Tech'	Stream 2 'Alpha-Active'	Stream 3 'Alpha-Lite'
Minimum time required	1 to 1.5 hours	1 to 1.5 hours	30 minutes
Teaching style	Abstract	Concrete	Relaxed
Recommended (age) group	15–18	11–14	Schools
Presentation tools*	Multimedia technology	Visual aids and drama	Story
Youth participation	Discussion	Activity	Exploration
Preparation level	High	High	Low

* Note: The presentation tools are not unbreakably linked to the teaching style. For example, imagine you wish to run the course for an older group of young people using the Alpha-Tech style, but do not have access to multimedia technology. No problem: it is perfectly possible to run the Alpha-Tech stream, using abstract teaching style and discussion, but using the visual aids and dramas from Alpha-Active to illustrate the talks. The reverse is also true: there is no reason why you can't use the video clips as illustrations on an Alpha-Active stream, if you feel video will appeal to the young people you are working with more than visual aids.

Guest manuals

Along with this Leaders' Manual Alpha International have also produced two guest manuals to aid in the running of Youth Alpha courses. The two manuals are aimed at younger youth (11–14 year-olds) and older youth (15+ year-olds) respectively. They have been substantially redesigned and redeveloped and are intended to be visually and textually as attractive and relevant as possible to young people.

Each manual contains basic outlines for all of the 15 Alpha talks. There are also suggested Bible readings, explanatory paragraphs covering key or tricky points, recommended reading lists, and other content intended to make the manuals a fun and stimulating read.

Churches running Youth Alpha have found that it is not realistic to give out the manuals for young people to take home on the first week and then expect them to faithfully remember to bring them back for each subsequent session.

One possible approach is to give out the manuals to the young people at the start of each session and then collect them in at the end. This means that each person can have their own manual, to make notes in or refer to, during each session, but is not overburdened with the responsibility of having to remember to bring it from home on every occasion.

Perhaps, the best way to use the current editions of the guest manuals is to treat them as gifts that can be given to the young people taking part, either at the beginning or at the end of the course. The design of the manuals should allow them to sit easily in a teenager's bedroom, among the magazines, CDs and posters, and the hope is that on odd occasions the teenager might flick through the manual and be reminded of something that they have learned or be challenged to dig a little bit deeper into the background or real life application of one of the Alpha sessions. If this approach is taken then it would be possible to download and print out basic talk outlines for each of the sessions from the CD ROM provided with this manual. That way the young people would have an outline to make notes on, should they choose to, during the session, and a manual to refer to at home when the opportunity presents itself.

Evaluation

Evaluation is both a process and an event and is an essential part of building an effective strategy. Statistics now show that churches that receive the most from Alpha courses and use the course most effectively are those that run the course time and time again. There is no reason why this shouldn't also be true of Youth Alpha courses. One reason for this is the ability to learn from the weaknesses of previous courses and gradually refine your methods time and again until you have the best possible set-up and presentation.

Through the process of planning and preparation, and then through the course itself, it is vital that you keep in touch with your team and ask them how they feel things are going.

Don't be afraid to ask the young people themselves. ('Did you find the last session helpful?' or 'What are you most enjoying about the course so far?')

At the end of the course invite the young people who have attended to fill in a simple evaluation sheet (see Appendix I)

Make the sheets anonymous to encourage honest feedback.

Encourage your Youth Alpha team, as well as your church leadership, prayer groups etc with any positive results of the evaluation.

Take time to reflect on the course and any subsequent feedback you receive. Consider if any criticism is valid and then use it to improve the next course. Allow enough time to discuss, pray, plan and implement any changes that need to be made before you run the course again.

SECTION III
PLANNING AND PREPARING

It appears to be one of the laws of the cosmos that in any given person the relationship between their administrative ability and their flair and passion to work with young people obeys some sort of inverse proportion law. As one side of the equation increases the other decreases – the greater the gifting and passion to work with young people, the more naturally disorganised. There are notable exceptions, of course, and if you are one of that weird and wonderful breed, youthworkers with a thing for order and detail, then I salute you. But as a rule those of us that devote our time and energy to working with young people struggle with crossing all the 't's and dotting all the 'i's, and are not naturally suited to administration.

Why a whole section on planning and preparation? What's more, planning and preparation starting six months (yes, six months!) in advance of the beginning of the course.

There are two key reasons why administration, or planning and preparation, for the Youth Alpha course is absolutely essential.

1. Image
Non-churchgoing teens often naturally assume that church and all church events are a shambles. After all a bunch of old ladies and feeble men are naturally going to have trouble organising a tea party let alone a dynamic, stimulating 15-session course. If we want to rock these young people's preconceptions right from the start, if we want to put on something that is dynamic and stimulating, and presents them with a life changing gospel message, then we have to face up to the fact that it is going to take hard work and serious planning.

2. Relationship
Relationship was the basis of Jesus' ministry and it has to be the basis of ours. Now you might be thinking that relationship with the young people and administration are on the opposite ends of the ministry spectrum, but you'd be wrong. The more work we do in advance of the course, the better prepared we and our team are, the more relaxed we'll be on the course itself and the more time we'll have for building friendships with the young people and making them feel valued and important.

Look through the rest of this section now, then come back to it and work through it thoroughly at the appropriate intervals before the start of your course and you will find that your hard graft gives God's Spirit a lot more room to work through you and through the sessions as the course progresses.

Planning – three to six months in advance

Checklist
- ❏ Spend some time with your congregation's leader discussing Youth Alpha.
- ❏ Make contact with a Youth Alpha Adviser.
- ❏ Register your Youth Alpha course.
- ❏ Decide what kind of course you want and who you might like to invite (see Strategy section).
- ❏ Begin to consider and explore possible venues, then book one (see Strategy section).
- ❏ Talk to your church treasurer about the money that will be needed to run the course.
- ❏ Select and book a venue for your weekend or day away (see later in the section).
- ❏ Consider whether you plan to have worship on your course.
- ❏ Start enthusing your youth team and existing young people (see Strategy section).
- ❏ Set the dates.

Spend some time with your congregation's leader discussing Youth Alpha

For any youth minister, volunteer or salaried, experienced or just passionate, the support of your church leadership is the absolute prerequisite for running a Youth Alpha course, whether on the church premises with the church youth group, off site with non-churched youth, or in a local school. For the course to be successful you will need the support and the resources of your church, their goodwill, their prayers and quite possibly their money. And if the course is successful it will have an impact on everybody, not just the youth. Your leader must share your vision and understand your plans if this is not to be a disaster.

Don't be content with a snatched conversation with your leader at the end of a service or as you bump into her in a hallway; make an appointment, turn up well prepared, pray together. If you can get your leader onside, really supporting you, then you're already ahead of the game.

Make contact with a Youth Alpha Adviser

Hundreds of Youth Alpha courses have already taken place around the world. If you take a moment to find the name of your local Youth Alpha Adviser (either by looking in the latest edition of *Alpha News* or visiting the Alpha website: alpha.org) you could find that they have invaluable help and advice to offer you. Apart from their own experience they might be able to direct you to a Youth Alpha conference or put you in contact with someone close to you who is already running a successful course. Chances are that a short chat with an adviser will save you loads of time and effort in the long run.

Register your Youth Alpha course

You can register by contacting your Alpha Office, completing the form in *Alpha News*, or completing the form on the web page alpha.org. Your course will then appear in the Alpha register both in *Alpha News* and on the internet, and anybody interested in a Youth Alpha course in your area can then be directed to you.

Talk to your church treasurer about the money that will be needed to run the course

It may be that you already have a youth budget to work with that you or one of your team administers, or it may be that your church provides the money (probably in very small quantities) only on a basis of need. In either case it will be worth talking to your church's treasurer well in advance of the start of your course. You are far more likely to receive a decent amount of financial support if you explain the needs and apply well in advance.

Consider whether you plan to have worship on your course

On adult Alpha worship is considered a viable part of the programme if the course is larger than 30 people. It is believed that this gives you a critical mass for singing songs without embarrassment.

Obviously, the dynamics for a Youth Alpha course are different. Only you will know if worship would be appropriate for your course, and if it is appropriate what kind of worship would be most natural. It will depend on the kind of young people you have on the course, the size and strength of your team, and whether you have a gifted worship leader available to you.

Should you decide on worship you will find two relevant pieces in the Practical Skills section. One focuses on the kind of worship that centres around instrument-led singing, and the other gives some ideas for more alternative ways of worshipping.

Set the dates

Most commonly Alpha courses run approximately following academic terms. This is especially appropriate for Youth Alpha courses where the majority of participants will be in some kind of full time education.

Therefore, when setting dates it is easiest to work back from Christmas to Summer for a course in the Autumn term; from Easter to Christmas for a course in the Spring term; and from Summer to Easter for a course in the Summer Term. The same process will clearly involve different seasons in the southern hemisphere.

- Remember to allow for a special kick-off event as an introduction to the course.
- Don't forget to schedule the team training events, Sessions 1 and 2 before the course, Session 3 just before the weekend or day away.
- If you think it likely many people will be going away for half-term consider stopping for a week.
- Ideally the weekend / day away should come after Week 5 and before Week 8.

Alpha Team Training 1	Leading Small Groups	_____
Alpha Team Training 2	Pastoral Care	
Special Introductory Event		_____
Alpha Week 1	Who Is Jesus?	_____
Alpha Week 2	Why Did Jesus Die?	_____
Alpha Week 3	How Can We Have Faith?	_____
Alpha Week 4	Why and How Do I Pray?	_____
Alpha Week 5	Why and How Should I Read the Bible?	_____
Alpha Week 6	How Does God Guide us?	_____
Alpha Team Training 3	Ministry	_____
Alpha Weekend / Day Away		_____
Alpha Week 7	How Can I Resist Evil?	_____
Alpha Week 8	Why and How Should I Tell Others?	_____
Alpha Week 9	Does God Heal Today?	_____
Alpha Week 10	What about the Church?	_____

(If you are planning to run Youth Alpha in a school please refer to the special notes later in this section.)

Planning – two months in advance

Checklist

- ❑ Select which of the three streams you plan to follow (see Strategy section).
- ❑ Put together your advertising materials and plan your campaign.
- ❑ Arrange the hire of any special equipment you might want to use (see Practical Skills).
- ❑ Make sure that the prayer support for the course is gearing up (see Practical Skills).
- ❑ Take time to decide what kind of an Introductory Event you will run.
- ❑ Book a venue for your Introductory Event if you are not using the usual venue.

- ❑ Arrange the hire of any equipment for your Introductory Event.
- ❑ Consider running a Youth Alpha taster/demo-session for your core youth (see Strategy section).

Put together your advertising materials

There is no doubt that most, if not all, of the young people who attend your course will come because of a personal contact and invitation. While a brochure, poster or invitation will not normally work on its own to bring someone to the course, well-produced advertising will certainly promote confidence and will make it much easier for young people to take the risk and extend the personal invitation.

Alpha International have produced postcards which can be used to give to youth. You need to decide if you will advertise your Introductory Event (see below) together with the rest of the course or if you will have separate flyers for this – perhaps aimed at a slightly different group. (The course advertising goes to those that you think might well consider signing up for the whole course and advertising for the Introductory Event goes to those who are more doubtful and might be scared off by the thought of all 15 sessions.)

Take time to decide what kind of Introductory Event you will run

The adult Alpha courses use a supper party as an introduction to the course. People can easily bring their friends into the relaxed atmosphere where they hear about the upcoming Alpha course and are offered a chance to sign-up.

An equivalent event might be useful as you start your Youth Alpha course. It might provide a half way stage for churched young people who might be worried about their friends' reaction to being invited to a 15 session course, but are happy to invite them to a one-off occasion, as well as for unchurched youth who could be understandably wary of committing to even beginning a course when they know very little of what would be involved.

The general format for an introductory event is to focus on the social and the fun, but to have a short presentation at an appropriate moment about the upcoming Youth Alpha course. The presentation could involve testimony and the first talk in the session material entitled, 'Is There More to Life than This?' Obviously this needs to be as interesting and relevant as possible. At the end of the presentation, and at the end of the event, flyers or invitations to the Youth Alpha course should be handed out and the opportunity given for those that are sure they want to do it to sign up on the spot.

Possibilities include:

- a nostalgia disco 70s, 80s, perhaps now even the 90s
- a computer games competition
- a sports competition: five-a-side football, table tennis, tennis, volleyball, basketball, skateboarding, blading . . . whatever appeals to your young people
- a club night with music, videos and non-alcoholic cocktails
- for younger groups a kind of 'It's a Knockout Competition' with loads of messy games
- a concert by a local band, or even a battle of the bands with a number of local youth bands
- a themed banquet
- A film night, with a recent blockbuster projected onto the biggest screen you can muster.

Only you know what budget and facilities you have available, and you have a better idea than anyone else of what will appeal to your target group. It is better to do something simple but do it well, than overreach and find that you don't have the resources to follow through and make it a success.

Book a venue for your Introductory Event if you are not using the usual venue

There is much to be said for using the same venue for your Introductory Event as you are going to use for the Youth Alpha course. It will make the venue familiar for the start of the course, and will lend a sense of continuity that should make it easier for young people, especially those still in doubt to come back. However, if you plan to hold a skateboarding and blading competition then your front room might not be the ideal location! If you plan to do something special that needs facilities not available at the venue you have booked for the rest of the course then you need to make enquiries and book the new venue now.

Preparation – four weeks in advance

Checklist

☐ Invite your team.

☐ Encourage team to read *Alpha - Questions of Life* and *Searching Issues*.

☐ Start applying yourself to the practical issues.

☐ Begin to promote your Introductory Event.

☐ Decide who will be the speaker for the Introductory Event.

☐ Choose people to give testimonies at the Introductory Event.

Invite your team

Alpha group leaders and helpers

This is absolutely key to the success of your Youth Alpha course. These are the people who will have contact week in week out with the young people who come along. Whether you intend to use your existing youth team, invite other new leaders from the wider church, or use other young people as leaders, there is one excellent rule of thumb to help you decide whether they are appropriate team members for the Youth Alpha course. It is known as the Alpha 'test'.

Ask yourself the question, 'Would I want my best non-Christian friend to get to know this person and talk to them about Christianity?' If the answer is 'no' then that person might not be ideal to be involved in this way in your Youth Alpha course.

For more information on inviting your team see the article on 'Using young leaders' in the Practical Skills section (pages 40–1).

Commitment

Your team need to be aware of the commitment involved in helping on Youth Alpha before they agree to take part. Be brave and advise the team up front that they are expected to commit to:

- the kick-off/special introductory event
- the 10 weeks of the course itself
- three team training sessions

- the weekend/day away
- possible social events with their group
- keeping in contact with the group when the course is over
- praying for each member of the group every day.

Start applying yourself to the practical issues

The chances are that when running a Youth Alpha course you will not have enough human resources to have a team to deal with the practical issues, separate from the team that is leading and helping in the small groups. This means that if you want to be sure that everyone has the necessary time and energy to focus on the members of their group you must be highly organised as regards the practical arrangements.

At this stage you must be considering what work will have to be done at each session and delegating responsibilities evenly around your team so that no one (especially not you) is too frantically busy to give the participants the time and attention they deserve. Consider:

- Who will set up your venue?
- Who will make sure all the necessary equipment is available and working when needed?
- How are you going to arrange for the food and drinks for each session?
- Who will be the timekeeper for the session?
- Who will clear up after the session?

In the 'General Information' section at the start of each stream there is also a list of jobs specific to that stream that could be delegated to team members.

Preparation – two weeks in advance

Checklist

- ❑ Hold Alpha Training 1, 'Leading Small Groups' for your team.
- ❑ Assign all leaders and helpers to their responsibilities.

Hold Alpha Team Training 1, 'Leading Small Groups'

Even if some or all of your team have plenty of experience in leading small groups of young people this training session is essential. There are two main reasons for this. Firstly, Youth Alpha small groups are not like other small groups, and secondly it is an important opportunity for the team to get to know one another, form together as a unit and focus and pray for the course that is coming up.

You can take much of the content of the training session from 'Small Groups' in the practical skills section of this guide. There are also Alpha training videos or audiotapes available and excellent books published about small group work with young people. (See *Young People and Small Groups*, Danny Brierley, Scripture Union Publishing, 1998.)

Note: If you feel that these sessions are going to be vital to the process of envisioning your team then you might consider holding them earlier.

Assign all leaders and helpers to their responsibilities

By this stage all of the team should know both whom they will be working with in their small groups and also what practical tasks they are responsible for.

Preparation – one week in advance

Checklist

- ❑ Hold Alpha Team Training 2, 'Pastoral Care'.
- ❑ Make final preparations for the first session of the course or your Introductory Event.
- ❑ Make an estimate of the number of participants for practical and catering purposes.

Hold Alpha Team Training 2, 'Pastoral Care'

You can take much of the content of the training session from Pastoral Care in the practical skills section of this guide. There are also Alpha training videos or audiotapes available and excellent books published about relational work with young people.

It would be good to get the teams to pray in their small groups before they go. If they have any names of young people that will be in their group they can start praying for them by name.

Make final preparations for the first session of the course or your kick-off event

Be sure to take time to sit down in this final week and think through step by step all that is going to happen at your first Youth Alpha session or event. Have you forgotten anything up until now? Is there anything you will need that you haven't made arrangements for?

Planning and preparing for Youth Alpha in Schools

Schools are a great place to run Youth Alpha. To think of mission to youth without thinking of schools is like planning an expedition to the South Pole without thinking about snow. So, congratulations on having the vision to be thinking of school as an important place to run a Youth Alpha course. If you are a student yourself, and thinking of running the course for your friends or for your CU, then that's fantastic!

The majority of your planning and preparation will follow the same lines as the other types of Youth Alpha courses and this section is not intended to take the place of what has gone before, you should still work through the above sections but use this as an extra guideline to make sure that you are on track.

Planning – six months to a year in advance

Checklist

❑ Serve and build relationships in the school.

Serve school and build relationships

If you believe that God is calling you to work in a school, and you feel that Youth Alpha could be the right thing, then start by serving the school, for example by helping an existing Christian Union or the head of Religious education. This may be enough, but after a while you may feel Youth Alpha would be helpful.

Planning – three to six months in advance

Checklist

❑ Make initial contact with the school regarding a Youth Alpha course.

Make initial contact with the school regarding a Youth Alpha course

Whether you are a student in the school yourself or a youth worker hoping to come in and run, or help to run, a course, you will need a key contact on the teaching staff of the school to back-up or sponsor your proposal.

A known Christian teacher is always the best first point of contact. They will be able to advise you of the atmosphere in the school towards Christianity and let you know what is already going on and what is needed or not needed. Obviously, if the headteacher or deputy headteacher is a Christian then this is the best place of all to start.

If there is no Christian teacher known to you at the school then the next best contact is to approach the head of Religious Education. If this is not possible, then approach the deputy head or the headteacher. Explain to them what it is you would like to do within the school and take their advice as to how you should proceed.

Planning – one term in advance

Checklist

- ☐ Supply information on the course to your key contact.
- ☐ Decide on the context of the course.
- ☐ Set the dates.

Supply information on the course to your key contact

Put together information on Alpha and on the subjects covered in Youth Alpha for your key contact. Don't start out giving too much information (teachers are too busy to plough through reams of detail) but make it clear that you will supply anything else that is requested, and answer any specific queries.

If your key contact does not have direct responsibility for Religious Education in the school suggest they pass the information onto the head of Religious Education or to the head or deputy headteacher.

Decide on the context of the course

You will have to decide if you are going to run the course as part of the Christian Union or any other Christian club or activity that meets, or whether it will be run separately. This is a decision that will require wisdom and tact if it is not to cause divisions and disagreement among the Christians of the school. It is essential that you talk it through carefully with the teachers and students who are already involved in running Christian activities in the school and if at all possible come to a consensus agreement on what the relationship will be between their activities and the Youth Alpha course.

Once you have decided on this point you need to think about when and where your course will take place:

- at what point in the school day?
- where on the school premises?

You will need to consider how much time will be needed for each session of the course, and what facilities you might need access to (OHP, TV and video) as well as where the participants will feel most relaxed and comfortable. (It is also possible that the school will offer you one time slot and one classroom and you will simply have to make the best of it.)

Set the dates

(See the main section on Planning and Preparation) The Alpha-Lite stream at the end of this guide condenses the course into eight sessions to allow for the limited time allowed by the length of many school terms. If you do not wish to condense the material in this way you can consider running the course over two terms but you should be aware that the break in continuity might mean a drop in numbers of participants.

Preparation – end of preceding term

Checklist

- ☐ Make up / send out your advertising flyers and posters.

Preparation – start of Youth Alpha term

Checklist

- ☐ All advertising up around school.
- ☐ Arrange announcements about the course in assemblies and elsewhere.

Planning and preparing for the weekend or day away

A weekend or a day? As you are deciding what kind of a Youth Alpha course you are going to run (see Strategy) you will also need to decide whether you are going to plan for a weekend or a day away as part of the course.

You may find that there are a number of reasons why an entire weekend away may not be appropriate for your course. These include:

- A lack of finances. It would be wrong to exclude anybody from the weekend because they can't pay, therefore you need to decide in advance whether you have the resources to help those that can't afford the full amount. If you cannot afford this then it is wiser to opt for a cheaper day out that is accessible to all.

- Lack of confidence. If you are working with unchurched youth then you may find that many parents (and many of the young people themselves) are quite understandably wary about trusting you to take everyone away for a whole weekend. Asking, 'Will they be brainwashed or inducted into some weird cult?' might seem like a joke to us, but could be a real concern for many. Obviously we should do all we can to dispel such fears by being open in all our planning and communicating carefully with parents and guardians, but we might have to admit that this is simply too big a barrier to overcome in one go. This might be especially true of a course run in a school. (Although, over years, as the school's trust and respect for you and the course grows they might actually be willing to endorse the weekend as of educational value. This has happened!)

If you decide that a weekend is not appropriate then a creatively planned and well run day away can still be a worthwhile event.

Planning – three to six months in advance

Checklist
- ☐ Set the dates.
- ☐ Select and book a venue for your weekend or day away.

Set the dates

Ideally the weekend or day away should take place between week 5 and week 8 of the course. As you choose your weekend bear in mind possible clashes: half-term holidays, a big school event like a fair or a play, key sporting occasions the youth won't want to miss.

Select and book a venue for your weekend or day away

This is a key decision and there are many resources available to help you find venues that cater for groups of young people.

One key consideration is cost. It is wonderful to go to a purpose-built youth venue with state of the art communications media and perhaps some outdoor activities thrown in as well. But if this is going to make the cost prohibitive for some of your young people it will defeat the object.

A well planned and well run weekend with young people sleeping on camping mattresses on the floor of a church hall or barn can have just as much effect and in some ways be even more memorable. Think through what the needs and desires of your group will be and try to match that with what they will be able to afford.

For a day away you have much greater flexibility. Although obviously you can't go too far, it is possibly still a good idea to get off site and go somewhere new and different. Think creatively.

Planning – two months in advance

Checklist

- ☐ Set programme for weekend or day.
- ☐ Invite any guests.
- ☐ Arrange transport.

Set programme for weekend or day

The programme should be worked out this far in advance to give you the time you will need to put into practice all of the good ideas that will come to you as you brainstorm how to make this weekend an unforgettable weekend for your young people! What follows is a very basic timetable for a Youth Alpha weekend and day. It is intended just to get you thinking about what might work well with your group and in the venue you have selected and booked.

Weekend timetable

Friday

6.30pm onwards	Arrive
8.00pm	Evening meal
9.00pm	Short opening session
Late	Activity – bonfire, midnight hike, swim or . . .

Saturday

8.30am	Breakfast
9.30am	Session 1 – Who Is the Holy Spirit?
10.30am	Break
11.00am	Session 2 – What Does the Holy Spirit Do? Small groups
1.00pm	Lunch
	Afternoon activities, sports, or visit to other attraction
4.15pm	Tea (for those who are starving)
5.00pm	Session 3 – How Can I Be Filled With the Holy Spirit?
7.00pm	Evening meal
8.00pm	Entertainment, a video, a talent show or . . .

Sunday

9.00am	Breakfast
10.00am	Small groups

	Session 4 – How Can I Make the Most of the Rest of My Life? Holy Communion
1.00pm	Lunch
	Travel home

Day away timetable

9.30am	Arrival and breakfast
10.30am	Session 1 and 2: Who Is the Holy Spirit? and What Does the Holy Spirit Do?
11.30am	Break
12.00am	Session 3: How Can I Be Filled with the Holy Spirit? Small groups
1.00pm	Lunch
	Afternoon activities, sports, or visit to another attraction
4.15pm	Tea (for those who are starving)
5.00pm	Session 4: How Can I Make the Most of the Rest of My Life? 7.00pm Entertainment, a video, talent show or . . . ?

Invite any guests

You might feel that you would like extra support and expertise for the weekend or day away. You might like to invite a guest speaker, a guest worship leader or another type of specialist to organise the activities and entertainment for the weekend or day. A local Youth Alpha Adviser might be able to help with some recommendations if you don't already have the contacts. Such people tend to be busy and you will need to book them up at least two months in advance.

Note: it can take time for young people to develop trust. If you are going to invite a guest you should be sure that the specialist gifts they bring more than compensate for any disruption of the group building process that has been occurring over the past weeks. It is essential that the guest not be considered an intruding stranger.

Arrange transport

Depending on the size of your course and the number you expect to travel to the weekend or day you might be able to get away with pooling the cars of adult leaders. However, if the group is likely to be larger you will need to hire other transport and it will need to be booked well in advance. If you want to keep your costs down (and we all do) it might be worth approaching other churches, youth organisations, or a local authority to see if you can find a cheap rental before you go direct to private rental firms or coach companies.

Please note: no financial saving is worth any kind of compromise on safety. You must vet all vehicles, drivers and insurance arrangements carefully before transporting young people.

Planning – one month in advance

Checklist

- ❏ Liaise with the venue:
  - Is bedding provided?
  - Technology – are TVs, videos, OHPs all available?
  - Catering arrangements – who provides the food, cooks and cleans up?
  - Facilities for sports and other activities – availability, extra costs etc.
- ❏ Start promoting the weekend or day on the course.
- ❏ Put together a pack for parents including:
  - Timetable of the weekend.
  - Contact numbers and address for venue and church leaders.
  - Parent release form (see Appendix II).
- ❏ Assign responsibilities to team for:
  - Catering (if not taken care of by venue).
  - Entertainment.
  - Sports activities or outings.

Planning – three weeks in advance

Checklist

- ❏ Take firm bookings from course participants including a deposit.
- ❏ Put together a pack for weekend or day-away participants.

Put together a pack for weekend or day-away participants

This should include all the information they will need to enjoy the weekend to the full. It should include a list of what they need to bring, exact details of where and when everyone is meeting, how they will travel, and exactly when and where they will be dropped off when the day or weekend is over.

The parents' pack can probably be sent home along with this one.

Planning – one week in advance

Checklist

- ❏ Pass on any last minute notices and information at the course night.
- ❏ Contact the venue with a final list of how many need to be catered for.
- ❏ Make a bedroom plan (weekend only).
- ❏ Make sure you have enough transport.
- ❏ Arrange who is responsible for the transport of all necessary equipment.
- ❏ Keep a tight account of who has paid and how much.

Make a bedroom plan (weekend only)

Doing a bedroom plan for a youth weekend is a work of art and before you start you have to remind yourself that you can't please everybody all of the time.

A few hints:

- Try to keep small groups together as much as possible.
- Make it clear from the outset that unmarried couples will not be allowed to sleep together.
- Try to spread leaders and other trusted individuals around evenly to keep things calm.

Enjoy your weekend or day away and watch God move.

SECTION IV
PRACTICAL SKILLS

Included here are a range of articles written by people who have been running Youth Alpha in different settings around the world.

Young people at the start of the twenty-first century

Their culture

If youth culture were an elastic band it would be at the point of snapping. There are two forces stretching it powerfully in two opposite directions.

Pulling one way is globalisation, straining towards a future, which in many cases has already arrived. Young people all over the world listen to the same music on the same electronic apparatus, wear the same branded clothes stitched in the same sweat shops in the same developing countries, watch the same movies at the same chains of multiplexes, laugh at the same jokes spoken by the same characters on the same syndicated sit-coms beamed and pulsed around the world by satellite and cable, and communicate instantaneously in Internet chat rooms, and via instant messaging services, with peers on the other side of the globe.

Pulling in the opposite direction is a proliferation of local subcultures fighting back against global uniformity. A consumer society produces a myriad of options to choose from and any class in any school in the Western world will be filled by a bewildering array of subgroups. These subgroups of young people define themselves and differentiate themselves by exactly which station on the global spectrum of popular music they listen to, which particular global brand of clothing they wear, and in precisely which order they prioritise issues like the environment, the importance of wealth, animal rights, spirituality, sporting prowess, beauty and global justice.

To be successful youth workers and pastors we must become students of youth culture, not necessarily in an academic sense, but certainly through observation and contemplation. We must become experts at watching and learning so that we can tailor our initiatives to the needs, values and lifestyles of the young people we are reaching out to. This is a job that must be done 'on location' where your young people are, as no two outposts of youth culture are exactly alike. However, while the outward manifestations of youth/adolescence are wonderfully varied there are a number of universals that are associated with this stage in life. What follows is a very basic look at some of the characteristics of adolescence.

There is a tendency to view change negatively. As the teenage years involve quite dramatic and comprehensive change, the assumption is automatically made that the teenage years are a 'nightmare' for all concerned. However, when given the time, space and freedom to express themselves, young people are often able to show incredible insight and sensitivity. They are full of great enthusiasm, boundless creativity and deep compassion. They can be wonderfully resourceful, honest and open.

Their lives

Young people experience enormous changes as they develop from children into adults. Sometimes a young person acts like an adult trapped in a child's body, sometimes like a child trapped in an adult's body. They may appear very mature at times but their maturity is likely to be erratic. At other times they may appear very young but that does not mean they are stupid.

Intellectual

Young people are moving from a 'concrete' way of thinking towards an ability to think in abstract ways. Concepts like sin, salvation and grace are typically presented and taught in churches in a style that requires the ability to think in the abstract.

The Youth Alpha material in this manual is split into streams. One of these streams attempts to present these concepts in a way that is more appropriate for young people not yet thinking abstractly, either because they are too young, or because they do not have the academic or intellectual resources to interact with the material in this way (Alpha-Active). This is very important in a culture that is increasingly visual and not book-focused. The other streams (Alpha-Tech and Alpha-Lite) assume a greater ability to think abstractly but still make sure that there is plenty of opportunity for discussion of other ideas. This emphasis on open discussion and exploring together is a key part of Alpha. It is especially important in today's youth culture, which is influenced by postmodernity and wary of any claim to absolute truth and of anybody who tries to force their view onto others.

Emotional and social

Young people are searching for identity, trying to discover who they are and what they can do. This search for identity involves experimentation (new behaviour, new role models etc). Young people sometimes experience big swings in their mood and temperament. An increasing number come from dysfunctional homes and might find it hard to empathise with other people. There is a tendency to cynicism. No wonder; they will have watched a quarter of a million adverts by the time they are 25!

The small group structure of Alpha gives young people a place on the course where they can relax, be cared for and practise their emotional and social development in a safe environment. Ideally, the Alpha small group is a place where the young people can find their identity, be accepted throughout their mood swings and be loved unconditionally. The fact that no-one is trying to sell them anything, or force their views onto them, might even temper their cynicism.

Spiritual

Those brought up and nurtured in the Christian faith will reassess and perhaps abandon old interpretations of Christian teaching as they move towards a more mature way of thinking. On a Youth Alpha course we can help their thought processes to mature by encouraging them to decide what is true for them personally as well as what they believe to be true about God.

There is a tendency for those from a non-Christian or unchurched background to formulate a personally-tailored religion by picking and choosing their favourite bits from the many options presented by the multi-faith world that surrounds them. They tend to suspect anyone's claims to truth and may see objective truth as either authoritarian or impossible. However, nearly every survey shows that while this new generation has rejected established religion, they are desperately hungry for spiritual reality, and open to a meeting with God.

Prayer and Youth Alpha

As with any activity undertaken by the church, your Youth Alpha course will only truly be successful if it is prayed for as much as possible, by as many people as possible and in an effective way. The aim of this article is to help you develop dynamic and effective prayer meetings as part of your Youth Alpha course.

We see throughout the Bible that prayer makes a difference. God seems to want to move only in response to the prayers of his people. We can see this clearly on a micro-scale in Genesis 25:21, where 'Jacob prayed to the Lord on behalf of his wife, because she was barren.' And we read that 'The Lord answered his prayer, and his wife Rebekah became pregnant.' We can also see this on a macro-scale in 2 Chronicles 7:13–14 where the Lord tells us that if we turn from our wicked ways, humble ourselves and pray then he will hear from heaven and heal our land. It's as though God says to us: 'If you do what you can do (ie pray), then I will do what only I can do.'

Therefore prayer at every level should be encouraged:

- Team members praying individually (daily) and in groups
- Team meeting and praying together weekly
- Corporate prayer at local church level

Corporate prayer, ie praying together in a larger group, can be encouraging and uplifting as we come to God together with the requests that we have. We see this in Matthew 18:20 where we are told: ' . . . where two or three come together in my name, there am I with them.' Jesus seems to say that there is a special power when we come together to pray, as we see in the verse before that: ' . . . I tell you that if two of you on earth agree about anything you ask for, it will be done for you by my father from heaven.' So praying together is encouraged.

Corporate prayer builds unity in the team as you unite around the common cause of Youth Alpha and focus on asking God for his blessing and help. It brings us together when we take one of God's promises and turn it back to him in prayer, for him to fulfil his word.

The more a team prays the better the Alpha courses they run are likely to be. The faith of the team will be built up each week as they see the prayers they have prayed being answered.

So what are we aiming to do in corporate prayer? The first thing we want to do is to touch the heart of God and so worship takes a central role in the prayer meetings. Worship is not just padding that fills in the time between one section of prayer and another, it is the time when we join together in attempting to gain a fresh understanding or appreciation of the heart of God as we ask him to help us in our situations. The second thing we aim to do in corporate prayer is to bring about change in response to our prayers, culminating in 'a healing of the land'; ie we want to see God coming back to the forefront of people's lives. Thirdly we want every activity we do to be prayer based. In the book of Acts it was the same people praying in chapter 1 verse 14 that were involved in the explosion of evangelism that took place in Acts 2. In a team prayer meeting for Youth Alpha, as we pray, we soon realise that we will be used in answer to our own prayers. Again, this builds up the faith of the individuals and of the team as a whole.

Over the last few years various models have been developed that work as effective ways of releasing people in a group to pray. These are best led from the front, and take different forms. A simple model to begin with is one person praying at a time out-loud, although this can be limiting in a larger group of people when we want to get as much prayer happening as possible. Another model is to get people to pray in small groups, of three or four, perhaps giving each person in the group a specific thing to pray for. You could do this by asking the group to number themselves and then from the front give a specific point to each number to pray for or they could each take a name of one of the teenagers in their group and pray for them.

In Acts 4 we hear that 'they raised their voices together in prayer'. This can be a great model to use. You could do this in one of two ways. You could separate your group in two and have one group praying out-loud together as the others worship and then swap over half way. Or you could simply all pray aloud together to God at the same time.

Sometimes we can sing our prayers to God. Many current worship songs are prayers anyway, and they can be great as a way of offering your requests to God in a different manner. Another powerful way can be to pray in silence together, again with a specific point for prayer in mind, and each offer it to God in the quietness of their own thoughts.

There may well be other models that you can develop. The main thing is to be creative and use a wide variety of models so that you can keep the prayer meeting dynamic and moving along.

As far as praying in your actual Alpha group it is always good to remember not to rush into it. If there are any unconverted people in the group they may not be comfortable with praying with the rest of the group in the first session!

The material on prayer in the talk 'Why and how should I pray?' is useful too when thinking about the subject of prayer. There is a hymn that is often quoted in the adult version of that talk: 'Satan trembles when he sees, the weakest Christian on his knees.' It is important to remember that the issues we are praying for are spiritual and real, and that our prayers have power – they make a difference!

Matt Hogg and Phil Dunn
Staff members at Holy Trinity Brompton
Involved in prayer, student and youth work

Putting together a team

A youth pastor in Australia has said, 'If I am the one who keeps bringing students to Christ, then we will only ever *add* to God's kingdom. But I believe he has called upon us to not just add, but to *multiply* the ministry of his kingdom, by equipping others to be passionate disciples and effective disciple makers.' (Tim Hawkins, *Fruit That Will Last*, 1999)

Putting together a Youth Alpha team that combines adults and young people gives us an ideal opportunity to do just that; we can multiply our ministry by training and equipping our students to be 'fishers of men and women'.

What does a Youth Alpha team consist of?

Set out below is one form of team structure. As every church has differing human resources, we need to be flexible.

Youth Alpha Team

- Overseer – one or two spiritually mature adults

- Speakers – two or three young people could help share the workload

- Small group discussion leaders – two young people for each group

- Small group helpers – also two young people for each group

- Extras – the team can build as the Lord equips. Intercessors, worship team games team, administration, social coordinator etc

Note: being 'on team' gives young people a sense of purpose, value and much needed community

Selecting the team

Reaching unchurched youth is about building relationship and trust and we must always be 100 per cent worthy of that trust. The people we select on team will either encourage this process or hinder it. How well an individual interacts with others will make a very big difference to the success of your course.

Having said this, one of the most exciting experiences is seeing the Lord work in the lives of young leaders, anointing them supernaturally with skills like compassion, understanding, love and patience.

> *'The Lord doesn't always call the qualified, but he will always qualify the called.'*

How do we know whom he has called?

1. Pray. Ask the Lord to show you who he wants. You'll be amazed how suddenly you keep bumping into the same young person or potential adult leader at the shops! Don't leave this till the last minute. Allow the Lord plenty of time to work in people's hearts; then they will often approach you with a burning desire to be involved.

2. A worshipper's heart. Look for people who love the Lord and ACTIVELY seek to please him. We're *not* going to find spiritually mature youth with a theology degree but we can find youth that are going for it. Look for people that the Lord is already working with, who worship him, actively seeking to change as they are convicted. Their passion for Jesus will shine among peers and this witness will have credibility among postmodern scepticism.

If we INVOLVE they will EVOLVE

3. Spiritual gifts. As the Lord reveals who should be on the team, spend time building friendship and trust with them and working out their gifts and weaknesses. Past courses have shown time and time again, that the Lord will provide the right people for the job and equip them to do it. If you're thinking, 'We have no one like that!', pray – you'll be surprised where they come from!

Finding their fit

Once you have worked out who should be on team, difficulty comes placing them in a role. 'Knowing' your team members will greatly help. Work with what the Lord has given you, he knows best. Here are some guidelines that may help, outlining each role and some useful attributes for that role.

The overseer

Role:

– To oversee administration

– To select, train and mentor young leaders

– To motivate the team.

Attributes:

– Adults who *have* biblical character as laid out in 1 Timothy 3:1–7.

– Are able to talk 'to' youth, not 'at' youth, able to release youth in ministry (not control).

– Are able to discipline youth, firmly but with love.

– Are committed to prayer and to time with leaders during the week.

Leadership style:

– A servant.

– A loving influencer and encourager.

– Patient, trustworthy, honest and reliable.

– Youth look for hypocrisy – they shouldn't find any!

– A motivator: young people need to stay focused. Remind them why they are doing this.

The speakers

Role:

– To prepare creative, relevant talks.

Attributes:

– People actively seeking biblical character (1 Timothy 3:1–7).

– Influencers: young people will listen to what they have to say as they have credibility.

– Committed: they need to be reliable in preparation, prayer, arriving on time and team work.

Adult speakers are usually needed for some of the more difficult subjects like 'How Can I Be Filled With the Holy Spirit?' and ' What About Evil?'. Adults need to put in extra preparation time to be 'current' in their illustrations, language and teaching style. Tape yourself and allow a young person to assess it for you.

Small group discussion leaders

Role:

– To facilitate discussion.

– Not to answer questions, but to raise the questions.

– Encouraging honesty about beliefs, so youth feel listened to, not preached to.

– To develop a culture of love, acceptance and an environment of trust in the group.

– To model prayer, Bible study and Christian disciplines as the course develops.

Attributes:

– Actively *seeking* biblical character (1 Timothy 3:1–7).

– Good listening skills.

– Confidence amongst peers.

– A good understanding of the gospel, but not necessarily all of the Bible.

Adults are sometimes needed in a small group but will instantly be treated as an 'authority' whenever they speak. Unchurched postmodern youth are suspicious of 'authority' and will tend to close up. Adults need to be very skilled in not giving their own opinion but drawing out others.

Small group helpers

Role:

– To get alongside one or two guests, love them, pray for them and walk with them through the course.

– To assist the leaders in the above 'roles' during group time.

– To be 'hosts' during hangout times.

– Watch carefully for quieter members of the group, making sure everyone is included.

– Welcoming people when they arrive, introducing people etc

Attributes:

– Self-forgetfulness in the presence of others.

– Networkers.

– Hospitable.

– Compassionate.

– Empathetic.

– Good listening skills.

The Lord is able to do immeasurably more than all we can ask or imagine, according to his power with in us . . .' (Ephesians 3:20).

You can do this! May the Lord bless your willingness to serve him.

Extra reading
Christian Youth Work – Mark Ashton and Phil Moon (Monarch Publications, 1995)
Fruit That Will Last – Tim Hawkins (Published in

Australia, crossfire@stpaulscastlehill.org.au)
www.youthalpha.org.au – Australia Youth Alpha website with lots of tips and ideas from Australian churches running the course successfully. Also has many links to sites about doing youth work and understanding postmodern youth.

Sally Irwin
National Youth Alpha Adviser, Australia

Using young leaders on Youth Alpha

Young people have passion, idealism, energy and belief. Do we see young people's passion, idealism, energy and belief in our churches?

A recent statement made about the church said that, 'If we continue at the present rate, by 2020 in some areas the church will no longer exist.' So, where have we gone wrong? What can we do to encourage church growth in youth culture? How do we develop young leaders?

Here are five principles for developing young leadership within Youth Alpha, and ultimately, the church:

1. Believe in your young people

We quickly realise that trying to be 'trendy' or 'culturally relevant' is a mistake. Culture is changing so fast it is impossible to keep up; as soon as you 'get it', 'it' changes again. Therefore the key for us is releasing the secrets of how to preach, lead worship, pray for healing, and run a small group to the young people themselves.

> 'I can now contemplate a music ministry course next year. Our youth leader encouraged us to lead worship when we were 13 and 14. Even though we were rubbish, he believed in us. It's given me confidence.' Katy (19)

So our job is to give away responsibility, to delegate but not abdicate. We encourage everybody to get involved in the course in one way or another. We say, 'Whatever you can do, we can make use of.' So, we use everybody: those who are good relaters, good organisers, artists, singers, dancers, speakers, musicians, technicians as much as we can.

2. Practise what you preach

Keep it real. A young person said to me, 'I went to a church recently and it was like they were speaking a different language!' The urgency for us as we run Youth Alpha is to demonstrate that faith and real life can work together. It means we should show that the subject of the talk affects people's daily lives. For instance, when we talk about healing, we must provide opportunity to demonstrate how it works. Jesus showed the disciples how to pray, stood with them while they had a go and then it became part of their practice.

3. Worship that works for youth

We often confuse two things: style and content. Think about your style of worship. Get worship right for youth. In nightclubs the DJs lead people. It's a worship-like experience to stand and watch the music move the people with the DJ 'conducting' the masses. Where are the DJs leading worship in our churches? Where there are the young people with these skills. Why not encourage the 'content' of worship in a 'style' that might be more natural for unchurched young people attending Youth Alpha? Didn't the Wesley boys steal the pub tunes of their day and put Christian lyrics to them . . . we call them hymns now!

4. Create an informal atmosphere for an informal culture

Do everything you can to help people relax. Lighting and music can be used to make a venue more welcoming. Plenty of opportunity to mingle is always included. Each session we include a 'What's God been doing?' slot. Lesley, one Alpha leader, got up on one occasion to tell what a painful and difficult time she had had with a bad back. It was a shocking and honest account of near devastation and isolation. About 10 people identified with the pain and hardship and came to ask Lesley to pray for them afterwards.

Release the micro-narrative – that's the small story with a big impact.

> 'I love to hear people's stories . . .' Dave (17)

Get young people to tell their stories. It's obvious really, but when did someone in your church last get up and say what a difficult week they had just had?

5. Make disciples

The structure of Youth Alpha gives you the opportunity to break the large into the small. Seek to encourage, disciple and reach others through the network of small groups. Young leaders have a key part to play in this process. The small groups give the personal touch. The young people can give support to each other, and encourage responsibility in leadership amongst peers.

Revd Si Jones
Founding Director, Ignite Church, London

Pastoring on Youth Alpha

'A new command I give you: Love one another. As I have loved you, so you must love one another. By this everyone will know that you are my disciples, if you love one another' (John 13:34–35).

Pastoring on the Youth Alpha course can be summarised in one word – LOVE. If love is the basis of all we do then we almost can't go wrong. Jesus himself showed us what pastoral care is all about with his disciples. Through love and his example to them he transformed a ragged bunch of 12 not-that-special-or-intelligent fishermen into the founders of his church on earth.

Aim

The aim of pastoral care is put simply in Colossians 1:28–29, that 'We proclaim him [Jesus], admonishing and teaching everyone with all wisdom, so that we may present everyone perfect in Christ. To this end I labour, struggling with all his energy, which so powerfully works in me.'

We want to see every teenager who comes on a Youth Alpha course welcomed, loved, appreciated, and above all, we want to see him or her come to know Jesus Christ! And we want to provide good follow-up so that they crack on and get involved in a church and mature as Christians.

But how?

On the course

The main way that we pastor youth on the Youth Alpha course is through the small groups. It's in the small groups that friendships are formed and the leaders can get to know the guests.

Get your leaders to divide up their small groups so that they each have a few guests to watch out for, and pray for. Our policy is that male leaders look out for male teenagers, and female leaders pastor female teenagers. This will mean that every guest will be welcomed and befriended each week, and the leader they know best will often be the one they can turn to for ministry or with any issues they have.

Some practical tips

- Make lists of the groups and divide them into smaller sections with the leaders and helpers looking out for a few each.
- Pray regularly for those on your list.
- Go out of your way to learn names and befriend them (avoiding all intensity or pressure of course – they are free to leave at any point so don't scare them away).
- Encourage them.

Follow-up

When they have, hopefully, become Christians, we also want to encourage them to grow as Christians – to stay involved in the church and a youth group – and in their personal lives.

Some practical tips

- Help them to get hold of a Bible.
- Take them along to your church or youth group meetings.
- Phone them during the week and say 'Hi'. (A great way to follow people up and encourage them after the course – but not at the beginning of the course as we promise not to harass them by phone.)
- Introduce them to Bible study – recommend some good notes.
- If they would like to, pray with them and ask them how they are doing.

One note of warning: in all of this we are aiming to point the teenagers towards JESUS. It is really easy for us to let them form attachments to (and then reliance upon) us as leaders. Looking back I know I've been in danger of falling into this trap myself in the past, but we need to pastor the youth in such a way that makes Jesus their centre, so that when we are not in the picture anymore they continue to move forward with him.

Leaders

It is also important that your leaders are supported pastorally, especially if they are teenagers themselves. Make sure that they know that you, or another more mature Christian are available for them to chat to if they would like, or if there are any issues arising that they may need help with.

Commit! We, as pastors, need to commit to what we are doing and give it the proper attention and time. There isn't much point in going into things half-heartedly. We need to commit to pray for the guests and our leaders. We need to be practical too, being sensible with time and making sure we get plenty of sleep are really important aspects of ministry. It is also our job to go out of our way to welcome everyone rather than just talking to those we know.

Above all remember love, and look forward to seeing what God can do! And trust that he will do things in the teenagers' lives, because he will. It really is a privilege for us to be involved in ministry with young people. It is so exciting seeing God begin to fulfil the potential in the teenagers we are working with. Enjoy yourselves.

Matt Costley
Youth Pastor, Holy Trinity Brompton

Leading Small Groups

Small group discussion

Young people face so many options and choices today. We need to help them make right decisions rather than just know the right answers. The church's traditional response has been to indoctrinate: to preach and try to yell its point of view louder than the rest of the world. This will no longer do.

Young people have 'information overload' from a variety of voices and messages. Most of these have a far greater impact than those they hear from the church. For much of the time they are told what to do, both at school and at home. They are not often actively encouraged to think for themselves. It is our task to teach young people *how* to think, not just *what* to think. We must equip them to make the right decisions *for themselves*.

There is no better way to encourage learning and discovery than through discussion. When young people are talking about a given subject, they are most likely thinking seriously about it and trying to understand it better. If young people are to make a meaningful response to the gospel, then we need to provide the necessary information and forum for logical and direct discussion. Discussion helps truth to rise to the surface. This makes it easier for young people to discover it for themselves.

We need to pray that their hearts and minds will be open to the Holy Spirit's guidance and prompting (John 16:13). We also need to pray for opportunities to show that the Bible can be their guide and that God does have something to say that applies to them.

Asking questions

Our main task as Youth Alpha leaders is to *light fires rather than fill buckets*. The best way to facilitate this is to ask questions. Questions help to stir imagination. Questions serve to broaden horizons. Questions provoke. Questions create a reaction.

Prepare and ask

- short uncomplicated questions. The best ones are, 'What do you think about . . . ?' or What do you feel about . . . ?'

- open questions (questions such as How? Why? What? that cannot be answered with a simple yes or no)
- questions that respect the value and opinions of the individual
- questions that point to the authority of Scripture.

Open questions

- allow a full range of answers; there is not necessarily one 'right' answer.
- allow every member of the group to chip in, not just the group theologians.
- help shy members to find their voice without fear of 'getting it wrong'.
- establish a pattern that all contributions are valid and to be encouraged.

Other helpful questions

- What other ways are there of thinking about this?
- Why do you think the Bible says this?
- What do you think this means?
- What other ideas do people have?
- How does this apply to your life?

Don't

- ask a question and then answer it yourself. This devalues the question you have just asked.
- put somebody else's answer into your own words: it invalidates their words.
- be afraid to challenge gently or to tease out a response. Eg 'Can you explain what you mean by that?' or 'Can you give an example?'
- be afraid of silence. Allow time for the group to think about questions/issues raised. Allowing silence shows that you value thoughtful and considered responses.

Do

- visualise the group as you prepare your questions. Make the questions as relevant to their world as possible.
- affirm responses equally, if possible. Eg 'Yes' or 'Thank you'. This shows you also welcome more responses from others.
- use questions to summarise and apply what you have studied.

Leader's role with the small group

- Become a 'facilitator'. A facilitator is simply another member of the group who is helping to make the discussion happen. We are not sitting in judgment on the young people or their responses. We are looking to guide and steer the group rather than dictate terms or indoctrinate the young people.
- Look for opinions not answers. Ask what the young people feel or think. This makes your question a matter of opinion rather than a matter of knowing the right answer.
- Foster an environment of open discussion. The young people will feel like it is their group. As a result they are much more likely to hold to what they have discovered and learnt.

Remember that ultimately we do not want to produce mere compliant, passive converts. We want to ignite and nurture active disciples, who will then go out and reach other people of their own accord.

A facilitator will

- affirm all legitimate opinions
- actively listen to each person
- not force anyone to talk
- not take sides during the discussion
- be creative and flexible . . . know what the goals are for each discussion/session
- briefly summarise key points that have been made

If the group tends to direct all their questions to you, affirm the questioner and then gently redirect the question back to the group: eg 'That's a thoughtful question, thank you. I wonder what some of you think?' or 'How would you attempt to answer that?'

Ground rules for an effective discussion

- No put-downs. Mutual respect is important. It is permissible for the group to attack ideas, but not each other.
- There's no such thing as a stupid question. It is vital that the young people feel free to ask questions at any time. Asking questions is an indication that they want to learn.
- No one is forced to talk and only one person talks at a time. This is a good way to teach young people mutual respect. If each person's opinion is worthwhile, it deserves to be heard.

Revd Tim Stilwell
Curate and Alpha Leader at Christ Church, Clifton, UK

Worship on Youth Alpha

Worship is key to what Alpha is all about – giving people the chance to meet Jesus. When I was 18 a friend convinced me to give my life to God and gave me a tape of worship music recorded at a gathering of about 10,000 young people. I remember putting the tape into my walkman and being blown away by the presence of God that seemed to fill my bedroom. That was the first time I experienced the Holy Spirit and I remain convinced of the importance of worship. It is a wonderful thing to be able to encourage worship on your Youth Alpha course. Here are a few pointers that might help you.

1. Pick someone young to lead worship

The ideal is for the worship to be led by a dedicated worship leader and teenagers will find it easier to relate to someone of their own age. It might well be worth the effort of training-up and resourcing a younger worship leader to serve their particular age-group and the Youth Alpha course. We need to try to identify teenagers and students with gifting and passion for worship, then pray for them, pastor them, teach them and resource them. This might involve allowing emerging leaders opportunities to serve alongside more established worship leaders, and to become involved in leading worship in home groups or cells.

2. Make the music relevant

Make sure that the songs that you are using are relevant to the young people taking part in the course. This will vary massively according to your particular context, but here are some general points that might help you:

Hymns

The majority of teenagers will have had negative experiences of hymn singing. Hymns might remind them of boring church services or of school assemblies. While hymns are important in the lives of many congregations they are best avoided when you first start introducing people to worship on Youth Alpha.

Rhythm

Most young people are into rhythm. The majority of today's popular music is strongly dependent on rhythm and it is a good idea to reflect this in our worship. Try to find a good percussion player or skilled drummer to play alongside the worship leader. As well as being skilled they must also be sensitive and willing to respond to leadership.

Song choice

Once again, try to tailor the songs that you use to the teenagers on the course. For example, some 11–14s will respond well to 'action songs'. At their best these can entertain, break the ice and also draw people into worship. These types of songs are very unlikely to appeal to older youth, however. Many sixteen year-olds (desperate to assert their own identity and maturity) would rather die than be seen waving their hands around or jumping up and down. Develop your song list with the help of the young people and be willing to delete anything they are not comfortable with (no matter how much you like it).

3. Character

The character of your worship leader is of vital importance. He or she must be able to work well with leadership, be open to being 'steered' and be open to the work of the Holy Spirit. As with the hidden keel of a boat, the unseen private life of the worship leader is more important than the visible/public part. It is essential that the worship leaders (especially if they are young themselves) are given the kind of pastoral support that they need.

4. Be yourself

Youth are very good at seeing straight through our clever plans and strategies. It is far better to be open, honest and up-front with them. If you want them to worship you must lead them, not patronise them or prod them forwards. Be yourself – no masks – and invite them to follow you as you enter into worship.

Al Gordon
Worship leader at Holy Trinity Brompton

Youth Alpha – alternative worship ideas

Worship doesn't have to mean singing!

There are lots of youth leaders who have had the experience of taking a group to a large event with a worship band and the group have loved it, but when they try to repeat the experience in the group disaster ensues. There aren't fantastic musicians, everyone seems self-conscious and nobody wants to sing, especially not the lads whose voices are in the midst of breaking. What worked in a large concert setting just doesn't translate to a small group. So the temptation is to think that worship and small groups are mutually exclusive. But this would be a big mistake. The challenge is finding things that work for your group and the key to finding them is throwing out your pre-conceptions and using a bit of imagination. Here are a few ideas to get you started.

Pay attention to the space you worship in

Try and make it conducive to prayer and worship by creating a vibe with ambient lighting and music, pictures/icons, and candles so that it feels like sacred space. As you use things in worship one week (for example say you played a video of surfing to focus on trusting God being like riding a wave) add them into the environment on other occasions. That way they become part of your worship language together (a bit like pulling out a familiar favourite song in church on the OHP!).

Use small rituals

- Lighting a candle is one of the oldest ways of praying. Put some 'nite lites' out and invite the group to light them when they pray. There are lots of variations on this simple idea.

- Put some stones in a back pack. Get each of the group to put it on and, as a way of giving their burdens to God, they can take it off and put it down.

- Write words of praise/thanks on post-it notes and put them on a board.

- Drink cool water as a sign of wanting God's refreshment.

- Have a bittersweet ritual where there is something sweet (eg dipping a breadstick in honey) and something bitter (eg pieces of lemon) and invite everyone to taste each and as they do to give thanks to God for the sweet/good things in life and to acknowledge the reality of difficulties/struggles. Accompany this with an appropriate piece of music (eg *Bittersweet Symphony* by The Verve).

Use everyday stuff

One problem with worship is that it is disconnected from the rest of our lives. If you can, use everyday stuff that your young people are into. They will be reminded of worship when they encounter that stuff elsewhere.

- Use their everyday music.
- Use images from popular culture and objects from everyday life.

Use pictures

We live in a visual culture so don't make the mistake of making worship all words. Find images that speak of God. One way of doing this is to have a week where you invite everyone to bring one image that speaks to them of God.

- Use old icons, contemporary paintings and photographs, or images of Christ from different cultures round the world.

- Give the young people a camera and invite them to try and take some pictures that can be used in worship.

- Try using video images. The key to video in worship is simple strong ideas rather than images that change all the time. Playing a simple video with a piece of music can be very powerful. Have the young people video waiting at a bus stop while you have a time of quiet to wait for God, or video a washing machine going round to play during a confession.

Use technology

Don't be afraid to use technology in worship.

- Try internet sites; perhaps the young people will revisit them from home.

Use music

Music really helps set a mood and can speak powerfully to people. Don't feel you need to use Christian artists. Use what works, makes sense, and the kind of music young people are already into. Some songs have a strong lyric that when used in worship can be brilliant. It can help to write a particular line or two out somewhere.

- Eg to focus on God's grace, play the track *Grace* by U2 and have the words 'grace finds beauty in ugly things' scrolling round a computer screensaver.

Use words

- Tell stories, rewrite psalms in your own words, write prayers.
- Invite people to imagine themselves at the scene of a gospel story and leave space for them to meet Jesus in it.
- Encourage the young people to use their everyday language rather than going all religious on you!

Worship somewhere else

Go outside, watch the stars, sit on the beach, go to a cathedral, visit a nightclub, shop at the mall and try and worship in all those different contexts.

Don't do all the work

A breakthrough will happen in worship if it's not all put together by you. Involve the young people in the process of putting the worship together as well as in the worship itself. That way you develop a language of worship that feels authentic because it comes out of the group.

Resources

Alternative Worship by Jonny Baker and Doug Gay (SPCK, 2003) has resources for creative worship and includes a CD ROM.
Multisensory Prayer by Sue Wallace (SU, 2000) has lots of practical ideas.
The Prodigal Project by Riddell, Pierson, and Kirkpatrick (SPCK, 2000) has a CD ROM with lots of ideas, pictures and stories.
Godzone by Mike Riddell (Lion, 1992) is great for stories.
Imaging the Word (Vols. 1, 2, 3) (United Church Publishing, 1994) have loads of fantastic visual liturgy images.
Images for worship (Vols. 1, 2, 3) (One Small Barking Dog) are three-hour long videos of images to use in worship (available from www.osbd.org)
Labyrinth Meditations CD (Proost) 11 tracks with ambient music and spoken meditations available from www.proost.co.uk.

Web sites to check out

www.freshworship.org
www.smallfire.org
www.proost.co.uk
www.embody.co.uk/archive/archive.html (a lot that is good but especially 25 safe experiential prayer exercises)
www.labyrinth.org.uk
www.the-scriptorium.org
www.trinity-bris.ac.uk/altw-faq
www.holyspace.org; www.osbd.org.

Jonny Baker
National Youth Coordinator, Church Mission Society
Member of Grace, an alternative worship community based in London

Giving a talk on Youth Alpha

To communicate the gospel so that young people understand what you mean is very exciting, but also very challenging. Your aim is to bring out the core of the subject in question with the help of video-clips, icebreakers and other creative aids. My aim here is to share some advice that it can be helpful to think through before you start your Youth Alpha course.

Make it short

- A young person is not able to listen to you as long as an adult. I usually have everything I'm going to say on one page of paper, and that is enough. If you have had experience of speaking at an ordinary Alpha course, you now have to think shorter, shorter and even shorter. This can be hard; it is easier to explain 'Why Jesus had to die' in 45 minutes, than to explain it in 15 minutes.

- Read the relevant chapter in *Alpha - Questions of Life* or watch the talk on video. This will give you a lot of background and act as a starting point. However, you must focus on the main points and concentrate on those, otherwise it will be too much for a talk in Youth Alpha. You can then move on to this manual for good, brief notes and outlines, and for ideas for illustrations.

Make it understandable

- Make use of illustrations, metaphors and examples. You can start with those in this manual, but remember that they have to communicate and relate to the teenagers in your group. If you are not sure of what you can use, start to relate to young people and study the youth culture around you.

- Make use of simple words and expressions that young people understand. The words that are familiar to you can be impossible to understand for a teenager. If you have to use 'Christian'

words like redemption, grace, sin, blood and repentance, explain them so that everyone understands their meaning.

- Be yourself. Don't try to talk in their language if that is not how you speak. Young people see right through such duplicity. It's not about being cool; it's about loving young people, drawing them closer to the kingdom of God.

- Make use of the Bible, but don't expect them to know anything about it. If you are going to let them read some verses from the Bible, explain to them how to use it. We usually start using Bibles for the first time when we talk about how to read the Bible.

Make it personal

- Make use of your own experiences in your teaching. Personal stories are often the ones that young people remember afterwards, so this is an important part of the talk. You can also let one of the other leaders or one of the teenagers in the group share something from their life. Just be sure that they don't talk for too long and check with them beforehand so that you know what they are going to say.

- Don't forget that you are an enormous example. They often don't remember what you say, but they will definitely remember what kind of a person you are and how you are living your life.

Sometimes you don't get that much of a response. That doesn't necessarily mean that you have given a bad talk. My experience is that a lot can happen in a person even if they don't immediately respond to your talk. The Holy Spirit works in their hearts even if we can't see it. If we do our best, then God does the rest.

Waldemar Sjögren
National Youth Alpha Adviser, Örebro, Sweden

Ministry on Youth Alpha

Professor Gordon Fee, a leading New Testament scholar, has written that, 'If the church is going to be effective in our postmodern world, we need to stop paying mere lip service to the Spirit and recapture St Paul's perspective: the Spirit as the experienced, empowering return of God's own personal presence in and among us . . .' (*Paul, the Spirit and the People of God*, Hodder & Stoughton, 1997, p.xv).

When it comes to leading ministry on Youth Alpha, we are essentially doing what Professor Gordon Fee advocates: inviting the Holy Spirit to touch young people's lives so that the truth of God's love for them isn't just something they know 'in their heads' but also 'in their hearts'. To use Professor Fee's terms, in times of ministry we experience the power and the person of God in our lives through the working of his Spirit amongst us. That is exciting!

But it can also perhaps seem a little daunting to us. 'How do I pray with a young person to experience more of God's love for them?' 'What if nothing seems to happen?' 'What if too much starts to happen?!' These are all very good questions that people sometimes ask. The aim of this section is to give you confidence in praying for someone following the model of prayer ministry used on Alpha and to flag up some of the pitfalls to avoid.

Does God want to use me?

I love the story of Moses leading the people of God across the Red Sea in Exodus 14. God tells Moses to stretch out his staff across the sea, and God says he will drive back the waters so the people can pass through. If I had been Moses I think I would have said to God, 'You don't need me to stretch out my staff across the sea. Why don't you just drive back the waters and I'll stand here looking cool and like I'm in charge.' But God asked Moses to do his bit – quite a simple bit really – and as he did, God did his bit – quite a hard bit really!

And with ministry, it is as though God says to us what he said to Moses. He asks us to stretch out a hand and place it on the person for whom we are praying and ask his Holy Spirit to come and minister to them (it's

one of the oldest prayers of the church, called the *epiclesis* – 'come Holy Spirit'). And just like Moses, as we do the bit we can do, offering to pray for someone, God amazingly does the bit only he can do, bringing healing, love, power, forgiveness, restoration, peace and so many other blessings into the life of the person for whom we are praying.

Yes but how?

When it comes to prayer ministry, the basic rule is *keep it simple and natural*. The Alpha model for ministry encourages us to be ourselves as we pray for others. So some top tips include:

- Ask the young person if they are happy for you to pray for them, and never pressurise them if they are not ready.

- If they are happy for you to pray, take a bit of time to find out what they would particularly like prayer for, and take a minute or two to sort out any difficulties of belief and assurance. Eg the person who says, 'I don't think God could love me after some of the things I've done', might be helped by the response, 'Well actually Jesus said he would never turn away anyone who comes to him, (John 6:37) and God has made forgiveness possible through the work of Christ on the Cross . . .'

- Explain how you are going to pray and encourage their faith (for example by giving them a promise from the Bible like the one mentioned above).

- Stay facing the person for whom you are praying, place a hand on their head or shoulder (NEVER on an inappropriate or sensitive part of their body, even if praying for physical healing) and ask the Holy Spirit to come. Keep your eyes open while you pray, having encouraged the person for whom you are praying to close their eyes.

- Silently ask the Spirit what to pray and be open to anything you feel the Spirit may be wanting to say or do. If you sense the Spirit prompting you to say anything particular, bear in mind that 1 Corinthians 14 tells us that the word of the Lord will be encouraging, strengthening and comforting. If what you sense fits that description it's probably from God, if it doesn't it probably isn't and keep it to yourself!

- After a few minutes ask them if they have felt anything in particular as you have prayed for them, again without pressurising them. I usually say something like, 'Did you feel anything particular going on as I prayed . . . it doesn't matter if you didn't . . .'

- Encourage them that God loves them whether they specifically sensed God doing anything in them or not (remember, we trust ultimately in the promises of God, not our emotional experiences).

- Encourage them that there will be more opportunities to receive prayer again if they would like to in the future.

Some final do's and don'ts

Do

- all that you can to maintain the dignity of the individual for whom you are praying

- have at least one person of the same sex praying with each individual

- explain everything as simply and naturally as possible

- keep in close touch with church leaders and parents

- encourage the young people with the promises of the Bible

- encourage them that the fruit God is looking for is long term character, not short term highs

Don't

- pressurise anyone into anything they don't feel ready for

- pray on your own for a young person of the opposite sex

- leave the room to pray individually with a young person even if of the same sex (ministry should be done in an open and appropriately visible way)

- touch individuals inappropriately

- be directive in what you pray for someone (eg 'God has told me you will one day marry X or Y . . .')

- give up! God does wonderful things as we offer to pray for people in this way week after week (assuming they want us to pray for them) but the effects are sometimes seen more in the long term rather than as a quick fix

Revd Jez Barnes
Curate Holy Trinity Brompton

Using the Bible in Youth Alpha

'There's nothing like the written Word of God for showing you the way to salvation through Christ Jesus. Every part of Scripture is God-breathed and useful one way or another – showing us truth, exposing our rebellion, correcting our mistakes, training us to live God's way. Through the word we are put together and shaped up for the tasks God has for us' (2 Timothy 3:15–16 The Message).

'The Bible is a high explosive. But it works in strange ways and no living man can tell or know how that book, in its journey through the world, has startled the individual soul in ten thousand different places into a new life, a new world, a new belief, a new conception, a new faith.' (Prime Minister Stanley Baldwin, quoted by Nicky Gumbel in *Alpha - Questions of Life*)

I think that we would all hold those two statements to be true, and cling to the Bible as our Father's precious gift to us: a way to know his mind and a means of entering into deeper and more profound relationship with him.

Alpha is a method of evangelism that holds the Bible as central. This is seen, not simply in the session 'Why and How Should I Read the Bible?', which affirms that the Bible is uniquely popular, powerful and precious, but also in the central role the Bible plays throughout the course. From the very first talk the Bible is seen as the central foundation for all that is taught.

Without doubt the 'sword of the Spirit' (Ephesians 6:17) is powerful. But like any other 'double-edged sword' (Hebrews 4:12) it must be wielded with care, and it is most effective when used correctly and with skill. It is perhaps particularly in work with today's young people that care is needed in the use of the Bible. First, we must be aware of the obvious: the Bible is a book, and many of today's young people are not at home in book culture. More specifically, it is essential that we are aware of the fact that few unchurched youth have been brought up with any concept of the Bible's

authority. Those who know anything about it at all would see it only as one holy book among many. It is very unlikely that they would see it as having any particular trustworthiness, and very unlikely indeed that they would see it as a helpful manual for teenage life in the 21st century.

Given this situation here are some very simple and practical guidelines for using the Bible on Youth Alpha.

- Take an opportunity early in the course to explain the Christian / your church's understanding of, and relationship, to the Bible. Clearly, you can't force this on the young people, but it is helpful for them to know that this is how you approach it.

- Always use a modern, easy-to-read translation. (Why not look out for opportunities to use a video, audio or comic strip style version of the Bible.)

- If the young people are handling Bibles for themselves do not give the impression that using the 'contents' page is inferior. Always give page numbers to help them find their way about.

- Do not assume *any* familiarity with the Bible, its culture, style, layout or well-known stories. Try to give a brief introduction to any passage of Scripture that you use.

- Do not assume that members of the group are happy to read aloud or, indeed, that they can read. If you want a group member to read aloud, always check privately first. Let the rest of the group know that you have done this. Then they will not worry that you might spring the next reading on them.

- If you believe the Bible is God's word, then trust God to speak through it by his Spirit. Resist the temptation to explain everything. Give God room to speak through the stories and teachings in a way that is contemporary and relevant.

Using technology on Youth Alpha

Fit to the culture

Many young people around the world have grown up around an extremely media-intensive culture. Therefore, it makes sense to try to utilise a range of technological tools in presenting Youth Alpha.

Know your audience

A first step when planning a Youth Alpha is to work out who your audience is. What music do they listen to? What movies or television programmes do they watch? Once you know the answers to some of these questions, then you will be able to start to relevantly plan the technological parts of your presentation. There is little point in using clips from videos that the young people have no interest in, even if you enjoyed them.

Tools you may wish to use

There are many different kinds of technologies that may be used in a Youth Alpha session. The following are some suggestions.

Powerpoint slides

Slides run directly from a computer using software such as *Microsoft Powerpoint*, *Corel Presentations* or similar, have numerous benefits over overhead transparencies. It minimises the danger of getting your pages out of order, and enables you to use more slides than transparencies allow. Also, you can easily integrate pictures, music and video clips into one package.

If you have one to use, project the slides using a laptop computer and data projector. A cheaper alternative that can work with groups of up to 40 is to use a scan converter to place slides from your computer onto a large screen television.

When designing slides:

- Use flashy 'bells and whistles' with care. While they might be fun to start with, 'clever' slide transitions with sound effects can very easily become tedious. Sometimes simpler is better.

- Make sure the text size is big enough to read easily.

- Run them through on the computer that you will be using to display them well in advance. Does everything look as you expected?

- Most presenters work on the use of one slide every two minutes. Too many, and the presentation can appear muddled; too few and it may appear a little static.

Video clips

Film or video clips are great for raising questions, setting up an issue or illustrating a point in a dramatic, visual way.

Before you use any clip:

- Check the film well in advance. Sometimes a clip is not always as you remember it! Is the content acceptable? Does it explain itself sufficiently out of the context of the whole movie? Somebody who has not seen the entire film might be a good sounding-board to check clips with.

- Make sure you (or one of the leaders) have full mastery of the technology before you use it. Is the clip cued? Can it be seen and heard clearly? Do you need to organise for somebody else to control lighting?

- Think carefully about how you will introduce the clip, and how you will follow it immediately afterwards. Don't explain the content of the clip – this will weaken its impact.

Copyright

Copyright law regarding the use of specific video clips is unclear. Film and video companies have advised that technically it is illegal to show all or part of a hired film to anyone other than your family. However, in practice the law is extremely difficult to interpret. As no one has ever been taken to court over this issue, there is no established precedent. Normally distribution companies do not mind clips of their films being shown as long as:

- it is only a tiny part of the whole film
- no money is changing hands
- no profit is being made

Music videos

Music videos from either secular or Christian bands can be used to illustrate a point or as part of a reflection time. It pays to get hold of and study a written copy of the lyrics before using any song (especially if using secular bands) to avoid any possible embarrassment.

The word on the street

Take a video camera out onto the street and do some quick interviews on the topic for the week. This can be particularly effective if you interview youths on their way home from school. Use the session names as the basis for questions.

Let the medium serve the message

Avoid getting so carried away with the technological side of your presentation that the message gets lost. Let the medium serve the message. It is immeasurably more important that a young person leave a Youth Alpha session with a clear realisation of whom Jesus is to them than see them leave impressed (or overwhelmed) by the visual bells and whistles.

Help! I can't do this!

Even the thought of being expected to try something vaguely 'technological' is enough to terrify some

prospective Youth Alpha leaders, but do not worry,

help may be at hand. I heard of a wonderful example recently where a reasonably technologically-savvy church leader was having trouble in projecting some Powerpoint slides. At the end of his tether, and having called on other adults to help, he eventually asked his 14-year-old son. The problem was solved in minutes.

The chances are that there is somebody in your youth group who has sufficient skills and would be more than happy to help on the preparation or technological side of things. Don't let the use of technological tools scare you away; perhaps it could even be a means to connect with some of your group's more 'techie' types.

Reminders

Know the equipment that you are using

Try everything out beforehand and give yourself plenty of time for any problems that you may encounter. The sight of somebody fiddling with television controls in the middle of a presentation can be very off-putting, as can be standing up to speak, only to discover that the bulb in the overhead projector has blown. Be prepared, and if need be, find somebody else to do the job.

Don't panic

Use technology as a tool to presenting a message rather than as a flash gizmo to attract a crowd. Become comfortable with what you are doing, and it will put everybody at ease.

Chris Darnell, Youth Alpha, New Zealand

Keeping safe and healthy on Youth Alpha

Working with young people is one of the most exciting roles anyone can have. But it is also one of the most responsible. In a split second, an accident or incident can seriously affect the well-being or safety of one of your young people or a member of the team.

Spotting anything that could put the health and safety of a young person or a member of the team at risk is vital. That is why some countries go so far as to make it a legal requirement for organisations and businesses to provide a safe environment. For instance, working with young people in England you might have responsibilities under the Health and Safety Act and the Child Protection Act (to name a couple). Are there policies like this where you are working? If so, what are their guidelines and how can you make sure you are working within them?

Below are nine areas that you might like to bear in mind as you plan your Youth Alpha course. Obviously, not all will apply to your situation and there is no need to be paranoid; equally, there is no excuse for being careless.

1. Risk assessment

It is a good idea to assess the potential risks of any location – be it a church building, a field, a conference centre, a beach, or a mountain – where you intend to gather a group of young people. If in doubt, check it out with others before making a decision.

2. First aid

It is good to have a qualified first-aider on your team (make sure everyone knows who they are), and a first-aid box that is easily accessible and stocked with all the basic equipment. An 'Accident and Incident Book' where all accidents and incidents are recorded – anything from a cut finger to a fight with kitchen knives – is useful if there is ever any complaint or query from parents or others.

3. Food hygiene

If you are going to be providing food on your course think through the basics of food hygiene – at least talk to an expert. Some of the vital issues are how to keep the kitchen and equipment clean and safe, how to prepare food using the right knives and chopping boards, how to store food safely and making sure hot drinks are carried properly.

4. Fire procedures

The whole team should know what to do if there is a fire. Always follow fire procedures if a fire alarm goes off, even if you know it is a false alarm. Keep fire exits clear and unlocked and keep extinguishers in their right place. Know how to use the fire alarms and how to turn them off or reset them if necessary.

5. Parental consent

Get written permission from parents or carers before you take young people anywhere away from your usual venue. Make sure parents know details. These details could be put in a letter with a tear-off slip for the parent to sign and give back to you. Do not take young people out without this permission.

6. Relevant information

Whenever you work with young people it is useful to have information about them. Keep this information on file so that whenever the young person is in your care, you have everything you need in case of an emergency. Information for the form could be their full name, address, phone number, date of birth, name of parent or carer, emergency contact number, any medical needs, any special dietary requirements and so on.

7. Transport

Minibus: everyone must have a seat and seat belts must be worn – this is law in some countries. Try and make sure an adult travels in the back with the young people.

Make sure your vehicle is working properly and that the insurance is properly covered.

8. Child protection

Stories of child abuse surround us. Sadly the church is often seen as part of the problem and not part of the solution. That makes it essential that we act responsibly. There should be basic guidelines to be followed by the team. Although we are used to working entirely on trust it is worth considering having all team members submit to a police check, to ensure that they have no record of child abuse. Many dioceses, church groups and youth organisations require this of youth groups working under their covering.

Make sure the team is clear about how to and who to express any concerns they may have about the possible neglect or abuse of a child in any way. As much as possible, make sure the team know who is with who and what they are doing at all times – be accountable to each other. Try not to work on your own with young people but always as part of a team (even if it is with only one other). Never take young people out or away with fewer than two of you. If you do have to work on your own for any reason, do it in public view, making sure there are other people around, keeping the door open. Basically, be aware of how your actions look to others. Don't become paranoid but you cannot to be too careful. These simple steps can help protect your young people and the staff team.

9. Confidentiality

DO promise a safe place to talk where you will not gossip about what you are told but NEVER promise complete secrecy. There may be things you need to pass on because a child's safety is possibly at risk.

Hopefully, the issues raised above will be a helpful starter in thinking through how to keep the young people and staff team you work with safe and healthy. With the excitement of youth work comes the responsibility, but with the responsibility also comes the reward.

Nikky Mungeam
Nikky has worked for many years in both the Christian church and the state youth work sectors

Using Youth Alpha in schools

Having built a relationship with a school, you now have a huge and exciting opportunity to impact every aspect of the school. The pupils you will be meeting on a regular basis are your initial potential audience, but a member of staff may also be involved in your meeting and each person you meet will know many others and have an influence in other areas of the school. Running Alpha within a school is like throwing a pebble into a huge pond . . . the ripples will reach right to the edge, even if you don't see them get there!

So where do you start? First you need to be clear about the practical details . . . Which room can you use? Will a member of staff be present? When is it free? How long do you have? What resources can you use (TV/video, whiteboard, OHP)? This requires a good contact within the school set-up.

Second you need to *let the pupils know what is going on*. Publicity can be done in a number of ways:

- **Pupils** – Alpha provides an easy way for young people to invite friends. It sounds less threatening than a 'Christian Union' and doesn't attract the same kind of reaction. Provide them with invitations, get those you know together to pray for their friends and who they could invite and help them to think about how to put God in the centre of doing that. Offers of free donuts/drink are always good incentives to bring people to Alpha and once hooked they often stay.

- **Posters** – These can go up wherever you are allowed to post them, and be placed inside registers to be read out to individual classes at registration. If pupils make them they will feel part of trying to make this new venture succeed. Make sure they include the relevant details about where and when.

- **Assemblies** – The format for assemblies varies from school to school, but most teachers are happy to allow guest speakers or pupils to come in. Be clear about how long you have and what your message is. Some schools are wary about an overtly Christian message from outside speakers,

so ensure you know what is allowed before you go in to talk. On the whole, a course that allows pupils the opportunity to explore Christianity seems to be met with approval.

Third, you need to be clear about *how you are going to use the time*. There are two obvious times for an Alpha group to meet – lunchtime or after school. Both involve meeting with pupils who have just finished lessons and will be tired as a result. There will be competition from other school activities whenever you meet and whilst you may get longer after school, pupils want to go home too! A 30–40 minute time-slot seems to be workable in most schools and a suggested breakdown of time would be:

0–10 min	Social time (eat and drink, chat and get to know each other)
10–15 min	Presentation of material
15–25 min	Discussion time
25–30 min	Social time (say goodbye, clear up, time for individuals)

If you have longer, you can include ice-breakers, video clips or more social time.

Half the time in the suggested timetable is spent being sociable and half actually focused on the Alpha material. This emphasis on social time allows you to build the relationships that allow people to ask questions and be open in a safe environment. Although the shortest time is spent on the presentation, the relevant parts will be picked up in the discussion time. It is important to remember that this is their break from school work and Alpha shouldn't be just another lesson. Social time at the end allows individuals to approach you without being vulnerable to their peers. It is also important that pupils are on time for the next lesson, the bus, their parents and that the classroom is left clean and tidy.

One of the problems encountered when running an Alpha course in school is the length of the school term. Finding 11 consecutive weeks in a school term is difficult. However, there is scope for combining some of the weeks without detracting from the material that makes Alpha, Alpha. (See the Alpha-Lite Stream for one approach to shortening the course.) Inevitably, few of those that start the course will be there for every session, but every time they do come, God is planting seeds that he can water and make grow – it's *his* course, not ours. They are *his* children, not ours.

Remember, *no two schools are the same* and no two groups in schools are the same. It may be more practical to run age-specific groups with the pupils in smaller groups where they can relate to one another. It is so important to gather as much information about the school, its pupils and the culture of the learning environment, so that you can prepare a programme that is targeted to the needs of that group. For example, your approach to a Christian school, with a significant focus on teaching Christian values, would differ from that of a mainstream school. You can tailor your programme to the school environment: an informal, discussion-oriented approach (see the Alpha-Lite Stream) might work in 'chilled-out' environments, whereas others may be more 'tuned in' to a programme that incorporates technology and PowerPoint presentations (see the Alpha-Tech Stream).

A helpful way of *providing continuity* throughout the Alpha course is to offer handouts for every session (see the Youth Alpha CD ROM). It may be helpful to give out mini-binders at the beginning of the course into which these handouts can be compiled. This may also provide an incentive to pupils to want to 'get the complete set'. This technique also enables those pupils that miss particular sessions to feel that they can return without having missed out completely.

Amanda Bruce
Administrator and youth team member, Trinity Church, Cheltenham

SECTION V
THE THREE STREAMS

TECH STREAM
SESSION OUTLINES

General introduction

Arrival atmospherics

These ideas are intended to ensure a live and exciting atmosphere for people to arrive into. The suggested environment is different for each session and intended to start the young people thinking down lines that relate to the session's subject matter.

There are ideas on

- using decor: how can the set-up of the room provoke thought?

- using displays: what quotes, photos, magazine covers might you put up?

- using video: what film, TV show, or video footage might you have playing?

- using computers: what game or activity might stimulate thought?

  (Note: searching the web as a group is sometimes suggested. This is obviously at the leader's discretion, and in all cases great caution will be needed. One option is for the leader to do the searching and then make suitable sites available offline in the 'history' or 'favourites' folder.)

- cueing the small groups: how might you prepare the small group areas?

- using music: is there music currently popular with your group that addresses the question that the session will be focusing on? Consider playing these songs as background music and putting up the words somewhere in the venue.

Your space and limited resources might make some or all of the above impossible. Alternatively, they might free you to do something far more effective and radical. The key is to use these ideas to stimulate your thinking, then build on them with your own creativity.
The goal is that

- no one feels at a loss when they first turn up at the session

- no one is left standing alone in a corner of the room not knowing what to do

- everyone has options; whether they choose to take part in something, join their small group immediately, or simply hang back and absorb what is going on

Introduction to session

This is your moment (no more than a minute or two) to warmly welcome the young people, put them at their ease by giving them a glimpse of what will be happening through the session, and whet their appetite by mentioning the topic to be covered and hinting at why it might be of interest and importance to them.

Getting to know one another – unpacking the box

On the adult Alpha course the small groups normally eat together at the start of the session. This gives an informal time to chat and get to know one another before the more directed discussion later on.

The first goal of these 'Unpacking the Box' small group times is to provide a focus for the small group that should make interaction between the members easier. The group leader should have plenty of opportunity to draw out the quiet members and encourage those who lack confidence. Don't rule out the food though. Depending on the timing of your course, the likes and dislikes of your participants, and the facilities available to you, you could provide a full meal with multiple courses and proper cutlery, or finger-foods like pizza, burgers and hot dogs. Even a few crisps and sweets – fruits and vegetables if you are health conscious – can have a positive effect.

The second goal is to continue the process of drawing the young people into the subject matter for the session. The simple fact is that most young people do not wander the streets or live their lives thinking about the big questions, or wondering what answers Christianity might provide to these. The questions exist but at a deeper level, more felt, less thought. The environment recommended in the 'Arrival Atmospherics' section should start the young people thinking along the right lines, and this 'Unpacking the Box' section should help them to formulate and begin to engage with the questions that the teaching will go on to address.

Teaching material

The adult Alpha course, based on Nicky Gumbel's book *Alpha - Questions of Life*, is a wide-ranging and in-depth introduction to the Christian faith. There is simply more material than it is possible to present to a group of young people in an equivalent number of sessions.

This stream, Alpha-Tech, is aimed at older or more academically motivated youth, and those that have previous experience of Christianity. Nonetheless, for the course to work the material must be reduced and simplified, without succumbing to the temptation to be simplistic.

The teaching outlines given here are not intended to substitute your personal knowledge of the Alpha course material. They are intended to give you ideas on how to present the material and to reduce your preparation time. For this stream the emphasis is on video clips and other multi-media or technological means of illustrating the points. We hope that we are providing you with more material and more illustrations than you would be likely to use in one session. Choose the material that you think is most relevant to your group, and the methods that will best aid you in presenting it to them in an engaging and relevant way. Throughout the outlines bullet points indicate what it is suggested the leader actually says – in your own words of course.

Note on video clips – at every point that we recommend using a video clip we briefly note the illustrative goal of the clip.

Once you have looked at the goal of the clip you might be able to think of clips from recent films familiar to you and the group that might be appropriate. Should you struggle to do this we have also provided one or two examples from well-known and widely available films if you can think of nothing better. It is strongly recommended that you view the clips carefully to be certain there is nothing that might cause offence to you or your group.

There are also a number of occasions when it will be useful to show dramatic scenes from film versions of the life of Jesus. You could take these scenes from any one of the following widely available video resources:

Jesus of Nazareth

The Jesus Video

The Miracle Maker

The Visual Bible

It might be worth your obtaining a catalogue from your local video rental store so that you can check availability without having to visit the shop and scour the shelves again and again. Alternatively, consider joining a mail-order or Internet video club and buying the videos. Many popular recent films can be bought for little more than the cost of a couple of nights rental and if you plan to run the course more than once, or use the clips in other settings, this might be an economic approach. Some Youth Alpha courses have negotiated beneficial terms with a local video shop, and even received special vouchers for the young people to use in the shop. It's worth a try!
(See the 'Using Technology' article in the Practical Skills section for more information.)

Discussion – in small groups

Small group discussion following the talk is an essential part of Alpha. It is a chance for the young people to express their views, and for their thoughts to be taken seriously and valued. It is also a chance for them to raise any questions they have about the talk, and to start to apply what has been said to their own lives.

Each session provides questions for the leader in order to stimulate discussion should stimulation be needed. From Session 2 onwards there is also an optional Bible study so that those groups that are ready for it can begin to engage with the Bible for themselves.

Other relevant questions that can be used on any of the sessions include:

- Is this a completely new subject for anyone?
- What did you feel about the talk?
- Did anything that was said particularly speak to you or surprise you?

Delegates specific responsibilities

Arrival atmospherics coordinator – to put together all that is needed and to set-up

Video clip monitor – to acquire the videos and cue them up for the sessions

Visual aid monitor – to put together and set-up equipment for the visual aids.

Introductory session – Is There More to Life than This?

Introduction

Start with some opinions about Christianity from local youth. (You could video some quick interviews with kids on the streets, or simply take Polaroid photos and project them on OHPs with brief quotes of what was said.)

- I'm young and this is the start of the 21st Century. What on earth does Christianity have to offer me?
- Over the next few minutes I would like to make a small start at answering that question.

1. Direction

Video clip – somebody setting out to change the course of their life

Bridget Jones: 46:12–47:56 when she resigns

Jerry Maguire: 27:42–31:14 when he walks out and takes secretary with him

The Truman Show: shot at the end when Truman leaves the 'set' for the real world

- Where are you headed?
- Not right now, not this moment, this week, this year or even this decade . . .
- Let's talk about the ultimate goal of your life, and even about what happens after death.
- Jesus said, 'I am the way' (John 14:6).
- With Jesus to show us the way we can have a life full of purpose and meaning – and fun!

2. Reality

Video clip – an example of the madness of the world

The Matrix: 24:45–28:10 (red/blue pill) and 37:20–42:05 (the construct) – how do we know what is reality?

City Slickers: Billy Crystal speech near the start about the meaninglessness and randomness of life

- It's a crazy mixed up world we live in.
- People are confused and many don't even know it.
- But what you believe matters. It determines the course of your life.
- Jesus said, 'I am the truth' (John 14:6).
- With Jesus to show us the truth we can make sense of the world around us.

3. Life

Video clip – somebody making a decision to go with good or evil

Return of the Jedi: 1:46:00–1:48:55 Luke and Darth battle and argue

Lord of the Rings: Boromir as he tries to steal the ring from Frodo

- It's dark out there.
- The world can be a dark place and the line between darkness and light passes through the heart of each of us.
- Every human has the potential to do good or to do evil with their lives.
- Jesus said, 'I am the life' (John 14:6).
- With Jesus we can turn our backs on evil, the dark side, and live forever in the light. (Emphasise life in the light at this point. Use personal testimony, or other illustrations. We want to finish here on a positive note; darkness is real, life can be hard, but with God it can be a beautiful, exciting adventure.)

Conclusion

- Christianity is not boring – it is about living life to the full.
- Christianity is not untrue – it is the truth.

- Christianity is not irrelevant – it transforms the whole of our lives.
- Don't listen to the lies

- Jesus can give you life
- Check it out for yourself

Session 1 – Who Is Jesus?

Arrival atmospherics

The environment for this session is intended to get the young people thinking about fame.

- Using displays: plaster the walls with photos/posters of famous people. Intersperse these with images of Jesus.
- Using video: play a recording of a TV celebrity gossip show.
- Using computers: search the web for sites devoted to the famous.
- Cueing the small groups: have celebrity gossip type magazines available on the group tables for the young people to look through and discuss.

Introduction to the session

As this is the first session take slightly longer over the introduction. Introduce Youth Alpha and explain a little of what will be happening throughout the course. Think of it as a bus journey. The group don't need to know the name of every street they pass, but they need to know the general direction they are going in.

- Welcome to this (evening's) session.
- Let me tell you a little about Youth Alpha . . . (whatever you feel they need to know).
- You might have noticed that fame is a key to this session. It matters in our society – some say it is the only thing that matters.
- Today we want to explore what sets Jesus of Nazareth apart from all other famous people.

Unpacking the box – in small groups

Famous quote from anonymous source:
'All the armies that ever marched, and all the navies that ever sailed, and all the parliaments that ever sat, and all the kings that ever reigned, put together have not affected the life of humans on earth as has that one solitary life.'

- Order this list according to the likelihood of their being the subject of the quote. (Add or subtract from this list according to the interests and knowledge of your group, and according to which 'stars' are currently the most talked about.)
- Hitler; Buddha; Nelson Mandela; Madonna; Mohammed; Tom Cruise; Jesus of Nazareth; Kylie Minogue; Julius Caesar; Christopher Columbus; David Beckham.
- You have probably guessed that the quote referred to Jesus of Nazareth.
- Now that you know 'who' the quote referred to, discuss whether you think it is true.

Teaching material

Introduction

- Why has the 'fame' of Jesus lasted 2000 years?
- We know very little about him (certainly by today's tabloid standards) but this basic biography is agreed by most scholars – Christians and non-Christians alike.

  A Jewish man who was born in Bethlehem in Judaea around 4 BC.

  Famous as a great teacher and miracle worker.

  Crucified by the Roman authorities.

  His followers believed he was the Son of God and that he rose from the dead, and they took the good news through the world.

- To understand why Jesus' fame has lasted we need more specific information. For that we turn to the New Testament of the Christian Bible.

1. Jesus was fully human

- He had a body, emotions and experiences just like ours.

  (Human body – John 4:6; Matthew 4:2; human emotions – Mark 11:15–17; Mark 10:21; John 11:32–36; human experiences – Mark 1:13; Luke 2:46–52; Mark 6:3; Luke 2:51)

Video clip – a character who claims to be, or is considered to be more than human:

Bicentennial Man: 1:46:00–1:49:00 the court decides the robot is immortal and so can't be considered human

- Most people are happy to think of Jesus as a good human teacher.
- The question that we must ask is, 'Was he more than human? Was he God?'

What did he say about himself?

- This wonderful, wise teacher also made outrageous claims about himself.

  I am the bread of life (John 6:35).
  I am the light of the world (John 8:12).
  I am the resurrection and the life (John 11:25–26).
  I am the way and the truth and the life (John 14:6).

  He claimed to be able to forgive sins (Mark 2:5).

  He claimed to be the one who would judge the world (Matthew 25:31–32, 40, 45).

  He claimed to be the Messiah (Mark 14:61–62).

  He claimed to be Son of God (Mark 14:61).

  He claimed to be God the Son (John 8:58; John 20:28; John 10:33).

- If he believed what he said, but wasn't in fact God, then he would have to be a mad man.

Video clip – a manipulative leader tells the people what they want to hear:
  Evita: 1:06:20–1:13:23 speeches from the balcony to crowd
  The Truman Show: Ed Harris character (Christof) choosing which shots of Truman to broadcast to the world

- If he didn't believe it but said it anyway (just to get influence over people) then he would be a bad man, a con man – like a politician who lies their way to power.
- So, why do we believe that Jesus was not a mad man or a con man but the one and only God man?

3. What evidence is there?

Video clip – a scene of Jesus in action, speaking, healing, or caring

- Jesus' claims were backed up by the most amazing human life that has ever been lived.

  by teaching – his words are the foundation of western civilisation (Matthew 5–7)

  by works – his actions were sometimes miraculous, always filled with love (John 10:37–38)

  by character – so perfect his worst enemies could find no dirt to throw back at him

- He also fulfilled incredible prophecies given hundreds of years before his birth.
- He was raised from the dead by God his Father.

Conclusion

- Few of those who are famous now will be remembered next year, let alone next century.
- Fashions, fads and crazes come and go, but 2000 years after Jesus lived not millions, but billions of people follow him.

Discussion in small groups

- If, earlier this week, your Religious Education teacher at school had asked you 'Who was Jesus?', what would you have replied? If he/she asked you again now would your answer have changed? In what way?
- If Jesus were a member of your group of friends today, what do you think he would say, and wear, and do?
- If you had a chance to meet Jesus how would you feel and what questions would you want to ask him?

Session 2 – Why Did Jesus Die?

Arrival atmospherics

The environment for this session is intended to get the young people thinking about, 'What is wrong with the world?'

- Using displays: put up charity posters that ask for help with fighting famine and other humanitarian crises.

- Using video: play a recording of the news or a documentary highlighting catastrophe, war or crime.

- Using computers: set the group to search the internet for answers to questions such as: Which is the poorest country in the world? Is crime rising or falling in our country?, or put on a sci-fi video game that shows an apocalyptic, terrible future.

- Cueing the small groups: scatter newspapers on the small group tables/areas.

Session introduction

- Welcome to this (evening's) session.

- One of the most important questions that any religion or philosophy has to answer is, 'What is wrong with the world?'

- An even more important question is, 'What can we do, or what has been done about it?'

- In this session we want to look at the Christian answer to both those questions.

Unpacking the box – in small groups

Draw a big circle onto the largest piece of paper you can find (from a flip chart, for example). Place this piece of paper on the table, or on the floor, in the middle of the group.

- The circle represents the world.

- Write (or draw pictures) in the circle to represent what is wrong with the world.

- You can look through the newspapers to find 'inspiration' – war, racism, crime, greed . . .

Give the young people a few minutes to do this.

- Now that we have a picture of what is wrong with the world, what do you think can be done about it?

- Around the circle write or draw some possible solutions.

    Connect them with arrows to the problem/wrong they address.

- Are these solutions effective?

- Will these solutions ever be enough to solve the world's problems?

Teaching material

Introduction

Video clip – A depiction of the crucifixion

- We said that we were going to look at what Christianity believes can be done, or has been done about the world's problems, and, believe it or not, you have just seen the answer.

- To understand how the brutal death of one man could be the answer to the world's problems we have to look at what the root of those problems might be.

1. The problem

- We humans have a problem – we have all done wrong. The Bible, and Christians who follow the Bible, call this sin (Romans 3:23).

- Today that word seems old-fashioned and needs explanation. (Explain sin in a manner that is understandable to your group.)

Distortion illustration

This illustration will work with a slide projector, a video projector, an OHP, or a video. Start off with a perfect image on the screen.

Then gradually tweak the focus controls (or in the case of the video the tracking controls) so that the image becomes more and more distorted.

If possible use an image of a person, and then repeat the illustration with an image of the world/nature.

- When God first made humans he made them perfectly – in his image. As people disobey God and do wrong (sin) the image becomes more and more blurred.
- When God made the world he made it perfect. He also gave humans authority to run the world. Human sin has also distorted the natural world.

2. The solution

Video clip – someone sacrifices her/himself to save others that they love:

> *Brokedown Palace*: 1:24:00–1:27:00 girl admits crime to see her friend pardoned
> *Vertical Limit*: 2:00–6:00 father sacrifices himself to save his children in climbing accident

- Every once in a while someone is noble enough to die or suffer for someone else. Usually it is for someone they love or someone they feel responsibility for. (Refer to the particular video clip you have just watched.)
- God loved us so much that he took our place, substituted himself for us, and suffered the results of our sin. Jesus' death on the cross took care of the results of sin once and for all (1 Peter 2:24).

3. The results

- Exactly how Jesus' death on the cross took care of sin is a mystery (Romans 3:21–26). However, the Bible, and Christians down the ages, have used different images as illustrations of the results of Jesus' death on the cross. (Under the heading 'The result' *Alpha - Questions of Life* (pages 46–51) describes four images. Use those that you feel are most appropriate to your group to describe the effect of Jesus' death on the cross.)

Conclusion

Video clip – of someone making a daring rescue:

> *The Princess Bride*: 42:20–43:20 when hero dives into quicksand in forest
> *The Mask of Zorro*: Zorro rescues peasants from hanging at the start of film
> *Robin Hood Prince of Thieves*: Robin rescuing Marion at the end of film

- Each of us was drowning in our sin – dirty, being sucked under, about to die and separated from the God who loves us, but God in Jesus came to our rescue.
- God has made a way for the results of our sin to be dealt with and for us to enter into relationship with him. If we believe that Jesus suffered on the cross for us and if we say sorry for the things that we have done wrong, (our sins) we can begin to know God (Galatians 2:20).
- Testimony
  This would perhaps be a good moment for a personal testimony. Your story, or better still the story of one of the young people, could take some theoretical concepts and bring them right down to earth and into the realities of the young people's lives.

Discussion in small groups

- How did watching the video of the crucifixion make you feel? What do you think about the cross?
- Is sin too old-fashioned and out of date a word to be useful today? What would you say if you had to explain sin to somebody without actually using the word 'sin'?
- Christians believe that Jesus had to die on the cross in order for you to be forgiven your sins. How do you feel about that?

Optional Bible study – in small groups

Read: Luke 15.11–24 The parable of the prodigal son

- What kind of life was the younger son looking for when he left home? (vv.11, 13)
- What did his life turn out to be like? (vv.13–15)
- Have any of you had similar disappointing experiences in your lives?
- What made him decide to head for home? (v.17)
- What does the response of the Father tell us about what God is like? (vv.20–24)

Session 3 – How Can We Have Faith?

Arrival atmospherics

The environment for this session is intended to get the young people thinking about truth claims.

- Using displays: put up pictures of mythical creatures – ET; Yetis; Loch Ness Monster . . .

- Using video: have an episode of the 'X-files' playing during the arrival time.

- Using computers: make available a 'whodunnit?' computer game, where the players must follow clues to decide what the truth is.

- Cueing the small groups: on the group tables/areas place a selection of urban myths/alien abduction stories / supernatural testimonies. The internet will be an excellent source for this kind of material as will the 'paranormal', 'unexplained' genre of magazines of which there are an ever increasing number of titles. Make sure that you read all of the material yourself before you make it available to the young people. You want to be sure there is nothing offensive, or occultic in the material.

Introduction to the session

- Welcome to this (evening's) session.

- I hope you've enjoyed the gallery of the bizarre and weird that we've prepared for you. The amazing thing is that there are people out there who believe everything that is on display.

- Today we are going to be looking at truth, and how we can be sure that our faith is real.

Unpacking the box – in small groups

Make sure that there are at least two or three urban myths / alien abduction stories / supernatural testimonies for the group to take a look at.

- Let's take a look at some of these stories.

- Which do you think is most believable / least believable.

- Why?

- Can we make a list of the kind of criteria we use to make a judgment about whether something is possibly true?

  (Eg credibility of the witness, our view of the world and the way it works, inconsistencies in the story, a better explanation.)

Teaching material

Introduction

- As we have just been discussing, it is difficult to assess other people's stories to know if they are true. Particularly if they are outside of what we consider normal or likely.

- We all have different experiences, so how can we be sure of our faith? (2 Corinthians 5:17)

- God is three persons in one – the Father, the Son and the Holy Spirit – we call this the Trinity. Each member of the Trinity – Father, Son and Holy Spirit – has a part to play in helping us to be sure of our faith.

1. What the Father promises

- It is safer to rely on God's promises in the Bible than on our changeable feelings.

- The Bible is the book of God the Father. It is full of his promises to us.

'I will come in' (Revelation 3:20) - he is waiting to start a relationship with us.

'I am always with you' (Matthew 28:20) - he never leaves us even for a moment.

'I give them eternal life' (John 10:28) - we have heaven to look forward to.

Video clip – someone taking a leap of faith:
  Golden Eye: 1:20–2:00 James Bond jumping off the dam

Vertical Limit: 1hr 38–40min leap across wide chasm

Indiana Jones and the Last Crusade: 1:42:30–1:44:24

- Faith has sometimes been defined as meaning: 'To lean your whole weight upon.'

- Faith = taking God's promises and daring to believe them.

2. What Jesus did

Video clip – a person saves someone through a unique power:

X Men: 1:17:23–1:24:38 Wolverine dies saving the girl's life

- The character Wolverine was special – because of what he was he could save the girl when she couldn't save herself. (Or link to the clip you used.) As we discussed in the first and second sessions Jesus was also unique. He saved us and made a relationship with God possible for us when we couldn't save ourselves.

- We can never earn God's forgiveness but Jesus died to destroy the barrier between God and us.

- God loves us and died to prove it (John 3:16).

- He took our sins upon himself (Isaiah 53:6; 2 Corinthians 5:21).

3. What the Spirit does

- Whenever someone becomes a Christian God's Holy Spirit comes to live within them (Romans 8:9).

Computer illustration

If you have a computer in the room where Youth Alpha takes place (or if you can bring in a portable) then use this illustration. Show the young people the computer operating in MS DOS mode. It is functioning perfectly well, albeit it is not a particularly attractive visual environment by today's standards. Now restart the computer in its usual 'Windows' mode.

- What changed was the operating system that the computer was running. The new visual operating systems like Windows are much more attractive than the old ones like DOS.

- When the Holy Spirit comes to live inside of us it

is like installing a new operating system into our lives.

- The Holy Spirit inside of us changes us from the inside out.
  Our character/personality (Galatians 5:22–23)
  Our relationship with God and other people

- The Holy Spirit inside of me also helps me to be sure that I am God's child (Romans 8:15–16).

Conclusion

- We can be sure that our faith is true.

- This is not arrogant or proud because we are not trusting in ourselves. We are trusting in God: his promises to us; his work to free us from sin; and his Holy Spirit changing us from the inside out (1 John 5:13).

Discussion in small groups

- What would you write if you had to fill in a questionnaire that asked, 'What is your religion?'

- Who or what do you have faith in? How do you feel about faith?

- The talk mentioned that being a Christian changes us – our personality and character. What sort of person would you really like to be?

- If you had to pick an animal that represented your relationship with God, which animal would you pick? For example: cheetah – racing on; ostrich – head stuck in the sand trying to ignore it all; dog – steady and dependable.

Optional Bible study – in small groups

Read: 1 Peter 1:3–8 Praise God for a living hope

- What do you think Peter means when he talks about a 'new birth'? (v.3)

- What do Christians have to look forward to? (vv.4–5)

- Should this affect the way we deal with difficulties in our lives? (vv.6–7)

- What does verse 8 tell us about the kind of relationship we can have with Jesus?

Session 4 – Why and How Do I Pray?

Arrival atmospherics

The environment for this session is intended to get the young people thinking about disasters. (Obviously you need to be sensitive if you have reason to believe that any of the group have recently suffered any particular trauma.)

- Using displays: put up pictures of volcanoes erupting, tidal waves, or dinosaurs (supposedly wiped out by a major disaster).

- Using video: play one of the big disaster movies that are so popular – *Volcano*; *Dante's Peak*; *Twister*; *Deep Impact*; *Titanic*.

- Using computers: run a game where the players must fight to avoid being overcome by a disaster.

Introduction to the session

- Welcome to this (evening's) session.

- You might have noticed the rather disaster ridden theme to the room when you arrived.

- Unfortunately disasters are part of life on earth. The key question is how we respond to them.

- The way humans respond to disasters is a starting point for what we are going to be looking at later in this session.

Unpacking the box – in small groups

Take this opportunity to talk through some of the natural human responses to disaster with your group. Consider the range of events that might qualify as disasters in the young people's lives, from the merely annoying (failing an exam or driving test); to the distressing (the end of an important relationship); to the genuinely tragic (losing one or more family members). You will need to be sensitive to the level of hurt in the stories shared, and be careful to keep the tone of the discussion appropriate.

- What are the greatest disasters that you have witnessed or experienced in your lives?

- Could you foresee the disaster coming? How?

- When the disaster was over, how did you feel?

- Did you need to blame somebody? Who did you blame?

Teaching material

Introduction

Video clip – clips where, in the face of disaster, the characters turn to prayer:
Deep Impact: the meteor is unstoppable there is nothing to do but pray

- Very large percentages of the population – even those who do not consider themselves believers – admit to this kind of praying.

- But is there more to prayer than that?

- Why and how do Christians pray (Matthew 6:5–13).

1. What is prayer?

Video clip – clips that show characters trying to pray unsuccessfully:
Meet the parents: 22:00–24:00 family comes to the table and say grace

- Prayer is the most important activity of our lives.

- It is like having a 'hot line' to God – you can speak to him anytime and any place.

- We pray:

    To the Father – God is our 'Dad' but he is also holy and powerful (Matthew 6:6).

    Through the Son – Jesus is always our way to God the Father (Ephesians 2:18).

    In the Holy Spirit – The Holy Spirit helps us to pray (Romans 8:26).

2. Why pray?

- Because it develops our relationship with God – friendship is about time spent together.

Imagine your girlfriend or boyfriend – if you have no communication, you have no relationship. (Before you disagree, let me point out that communication doesn't just mean talking – you might get by without talking, but you will certainly be communicating in other ways!) If we don't communicate with God our relationship with him will stagnate and eventually die.

- Because we are to copy Jesus – and he prayed a lot (Mark 1:35; Luke 6:12, 9:18, 28, 11:1).

- Because it brings us joy and peace – even in difficult times (John 16:24; Philippians 4:6–7).

- Because it changes situations – prayer works (Matthew 7:7–11).

3. Does God always answer my prayers?

Reception illustration

Make the point that the air seems clear and empty to us, but we know that it us actually full of signals. (You could use a portable radio to show the presence of radio waves or a television aerial to show that TV signals are being transmitted). Mobile phones even have a meter icon to tell you how good reception is. This is because certain things can interfere with reception and transmission. It is the same with prayer.

- We can let things create a barrier between us and God

    – if we are disobedient (1 John 3:21–22)

    – if we don't forgive (Matthew 6:14–15)

    – if we haven't told God about the things we have done wrong (Isaiah 59:2)

    – if our motives are wrong (James 4:2–3)

- Sometimes we want things that are not good for us – God will only give us what is best for us (Matthew 7:11)

- Remember that 'Yes' 'No' and 'Wait' are all answers

4. How do we pray?
- To help us to pray we can follow a pattern:

    T   Thank you – praise God for all he has given you

    S   Sorry – admit to God what you have done wrong

    P   Please – ask God for what you and others need

- You can pray anytime and any place, while doing anything (1 Thessalonians 5:17). But . . . it is good to have a regular time when you can pray alone and not be distracted (Matthew 6:6), and times when you can learn to pray with other people (Matthew 18:19).

Discussion in small groups
- Do you pray? Would you consider trying prayer?

- Do you find it hard to imagine God actually answering prayer?

- Have you ever seen answers to prayer, or coincidences that happened after you prayed?

- What do you find most attractive about the idea of prayer?

Optional Bible study – in small groups
Read: Matthew 6:5–13 The Lord's Prayer

- Why does Jesus think that private praying is often better than public praying? (vv.5–6)

- From looking at the prayer that Jesus taught us, what kind of things do you think it is right to ask God to give us? (vv.9–13)

As the leader, take some time to talk about answers to prayer that you have seen in your life. Then encourage other members of the group to tell of any they have experienced.

Session 5 – Why and How Should I Read the Bible?

Arrival atmospherics

The environment for this session is intended to get the young people thinking about communication.

- Using displays: put up pictures related to different forms of communication: writing, TV, sign language, radio, Morse Code, flags, telephone, e-mail . . . the list is endless.

- Using video: play a film with subtitles or a programme with sign-interpretation for the deaf.

- Using computers: have the group list the methods of input and output. How do we communicate to the computer and how does it communicate back?

- Cueing the small groups: in the group areas / tables place things that are related to different styles of stories and storytelling. For example, a novel, soap opera digests from TV magazines, film reviews, children's books or magazines.

Session introduction

- Welcome to this (evening's) session.

- Today we are looking at / thinking about communication.

- Particularly, the primary way that God chooses to communicate with us.

- That key method of communication between God and us is the Bible.

Unpacking the box – in small groups

Have the group spend a few minutes focusing on the story related material that is in the group area. Keep the talk going with some questions similar to those below.

- Have you seen any of the films reviewed? Were they good/bad/indifferent?

- Do you watch any of the soap operas? Which ones have you hooked?

- Did you like stories as a child? Do you ever read / tell them to little children now?

When the interest has died out redirect the discussion by asking more analytical questions about what makes a good story.

- Why do you prefer film X to film Y?

- What is it about that soap opera that really has you gripped?

- Why do you think little children love stories so much?

Teaching material

Introduction

You will need a *Guinness Book of Records* best-seller list – or other.

- Put these books in order of biggest sellers of all time.

- No doubt you guessed right from the beginning that the Bible would turn out to be the biggest seller of all time.

- As well as being the most popular book in the world, it is also the most powerful. Many people have had their lives changed by reading the Bible.

- As well as being the most popular and the most powerful, it is also the most precious. You might only use yours to press flowers and prop open doors but there are millions of people around the world who would not swap theirs even for . . . (highly desirable teen possession).

- In the small groups we were discussing stories. The Bible is, above all, a story and full of stories. It is one story, the story of God and his love for the world he made and the humans who live in it. And it is full of stories about amazing people and events. All the elements that make soap operas and films so gripping are in the Bible. There is romance, war, revenge, love, sacrifice, murder, sex, and there are parts that would have the film censors reaching for the scissors to make cuts.

- Key fact: this is no ordinary book. The Bible is uniquely God's book. The Bible is 'God-breathed' or 'God-inspired'. Even though humans wrote the words, it was God who inspired and guided them (2 Timothy 3:15–17).

1. An instruction manual for life

Video clip – of groups of people being given important instructions:

for example: team in *Armageddon*; army drills

- We all need instruction – not everything comes naturally.

- Because God created us he knows what is best for us, how we can get the best out of life.
The Bible can correct us when we are living wrongly.
The Bible can show us how to live for God.

2. A way to relationship

Text message illustration

Arrange beforehand for someone to text a message to someone else's phone at this point in the talk. A good message would be 'I love you' but this is at your discretion depending on the group.

- If the Bible were just an instruction manual, it might seem a bit cold and boring like a very big, very thick textbook.

- But written communications can also lead to real relationship. Refer back to the text message, also to relationships built on e-mail like in the film *You've Got Mail!* The Bible is the key way God speaks to us and builds relationship with us.

- God speaks through the Bible before we are Christians to bring us to salvation through faith in Jesus (Romans 10:17; John 20:31).

- When we are Christians God speaks through the Bible to build the relationship.

3. How do we hear God speak through the Bible?

Video clip – scene in which key message cannot be transmitted because of noise:

Jerry Maguire: when Jerry's trying to get through to his clients and the agency beats him to them – their phones are always engaged

The Hunt for Red October: the scene where the American sub is trying to detect the – supposedly silent – Russian sub. One of the US crew records the sound of the ocean, removes the background noise, and slows the tape down – and you can hear a clacking noise that is the Soviet sub. Shows that the message is there but we have to be in tune to it

- In any form of communication the right conditions are important.

- Here are some ways to set up the right conditions to hear God speak through the Bible.

  Choose a time when you are not rushed or stressed – if possible make this a regular habit.

  Choose a place where you are relaxed and where you won't be disturbed (Mark 1:35).

  Begin by praying: ask God to speak to you through what you read.

  Don't just switch off and let your mind wander. Ask yourself: What does this say?

  What does this mean? How should this affect me?

  Put what you have read and learned into practice (Matthew 7:24).

- The Bible: read it, learn from it, but most of all enjoy it.

Discussion in small groups

Have to hand at least two translations of the Bible. One should be a traditional translation such as the King James Version, and the other should be a modern, accessible translation. Have the young people read out segments from the different translations.

- What do you think of those two Bibles?

- Have you ever read the Bible before? What was your experience like?

- Do you think that the Bible has anything helpful to say to you?

- Can it guide you in the way you live your life today?

Optional Bible study – in small groups

Read: Mark 4:1–8 and 13–20 The parable of the sower

- This is a parable. Jesus used stories like this to make points about how people live their lives. One key to understanding this parable is to realise that Jesus is not talking about different groups of people, but about the different ways we respond at different times in our lives.

- How do you see yourself responding at this stage in your life?

- Have you ever known God was talking to you but not done anything about it? (v.15)

- What sort of things distract you from God at different times in your life? (vv.18–19)

- What does Jesus promise to those who hear his words and actually do something about it? (v.20)

Session 6 – How Does God Guide us?

Arrival atmospherics

The environment for this session is intended to get the young people thinking about decisions and about guidance.

- Using displays: put up pictures of methods of guidance – maps; compasses; road signs.

- Using video: play a video of sporting or other bloopers. You can turn this into a game by playing the first few seconds of each clip and then pausing the video to ask 'What happens next?' Guessing what will happen is predicting the future.

- Using computers: use maps and guides found on the internet to decide where you want to go. Then have the group plan – flights, hotels, excursions – a perfect group holiday.

- Cueing the small groups: in the small group areas place pictures cut out from magazines and other sources that present young people (aged up to 30, perhaps) in ways that relate to their chosen lifestyles – ie their careers, their interests, their home life (partners, children, dog!).

Introduction to the session

- Welcome to this (evening's) session.

- Today we are going to be looking at decisions, choices and guidance.

- In particular, we will look later at how God can guide us.

Unpacking the box – in small groups

Have the group spend a few minutes examining the pictures that have been torn out of the magazines/newspapers. Then ask of each picture:

- What kind of life does this person have?

Now hand out pens and paper to the group.

- Where do you think you'll be when you are 30? For example: Who will your friends be? What kind of career will you have? What kind of life will you lead? Will you be happy? Where will you live? Who will you be living with? What will your ambitions be?

- On the piece of paper write or draw your life at 30.

After a few minutes, give each person a moment to talk about their piece of paper.
Next you want to focus on how they got there.

- Let's make a list of the decisions to get you from where you are now to where you want to be when you are 30.

- What will be your main sources of guidance in making those different decisions?

Teaching material

Introduction

Video clip – A clear example of guidance:
> *Star Wars*: Luke is guided in by 'the force'
> *The Matrix*: 11:55–15:36 Neo is guided by the phone in the office building (wouldn't it be wonderful if guidance was like that, if life was like that!)

- Guidance is typically more of a process – God promises to guide us when we ask him.

- God has a good plan for each of us (Jeremiah 29:11; Romans 12:2).

- He wants to help us to find our way in that plan and become all that we can be (Psalms 32:8; John 10:3–4).

- It is wise to involve God in all of our big decisions (Isaiah 30:1–2).

- Without God we are likely to get into a mess.

- God guides us in many different ways.

1. Through the Bible

- The Bible is full of general guidelines about how we should live our lives – we should always follow these (2 Timothy 3:16).

- God also speaks to us through the Bible about specific situations.

- If we make a habit of studying the Bible regularly

then God will often bring a particular verse to light just at the right time to help guide us in a decision (Psalm 119:105, 130–133).

Personal testimony – insert a personal testimony of God guiding through the Bible.

2. Through the Holy Spirit

Recording illustration

Make a sound recording of someone famous, and well known by the group. (It could be a DJ recorded off the radio, or any personality recorded off the TV.) Play the recording of the voice to the group, and ask the group to identify it.

- We can learn to recognise the voices of the famous, but we all know the voices of those we love. They are the people who can genuinely get away with just saying, 'It's me!' when they phone you.
- The Holy Spirit helps us to recognise God's voice.
- God speaks to us as we pray (Acts 13:1–3).
- Sometimes he speaks through our feelings, desires or thoughts (Philippians 2:13).
- Sometimes he speaks in more unusual ways: prophecy (Acts 11:27), dreams (Matthew 1:20), visions (Acts 16:10), angels (Genesis 18), audible voices (1 Samuel 3:4–14).

3. Through common sense
- God wants us to use our brains to think about the consequences of our choices (Psalm 32:8–9).

4. Through advice from others
- The wiser you are the more aware you will be that you need help to make the most of life (Proverbs 12:15; 15:22; 20:18).

5. Through circumstances
Video clip – where circumstances make it clear what is the best course of action:
   Chariots of Fire: 55:10–56:50 Eric tells his sister, 'God made me fast!'

Lord of the Rings: Gandalf's speech in Moria – 'You were meant to find the ring. No-one can choose their circumstances, but we must make the best of the times that are given to us.'
- Our eyes should be open to opportunities and to closed doors. But sometimes we need to keep going in spite of difficulty (Proverbs 16:9).

Conclusion
Video clip – after a long search the hero finally reaches the treasure:
   Tomb Raider: 1:13:00–1:16:00 Lara finally gets hold of the Triangle
- Don't rush decisions – sometimes we have to wait for God to lead us to the treasure.
- Remember that we all make mistakes but that God forgives (Joel 2:25).

Discussion in small groups
- How do you feel about the idea of being guided by God? (Do you feel humiliated like a dog on a lead or set free like the hero with the latest high-tech super-sophisticated guidance system?)
- Do you think you are on course to make the best of your life?
- What should we do if we believe we have made a mess of our lives?
- Do you think God speaks to people today? Have you any experience of this?

Optional Bible study – in small groups
Read: Proverbs 16:1–9 Commit to the Lord whatever you do

- What must we do if we want God to guide us? (vv.3, 5 and 7)
- What does God promise to those that try to live according to his plans? (vv.6–8)
- Does the experience of the group show that things go better when we live God's way?
- Can anyone give examples of God's blessing?

Weekend away: Talk 1 – Who Is the Holy Spirit?

Note: It is assumed that these talks will take place on a day or weekend away. Therefore, the usual session outlines are not appropriate, because much of what happens will depend on the type of weekend you are running and your schedule. What follows are the talk outlines and one set of discussion/Bible study questions designed to follow the 'What Does the Holy Spirit Do?' talk. (Over the weekend, there are usually small groups after this talk and before the final session – but the small group time before the final session is intended to be an opportunity to discuss and reflect upon the group's experiences.)

Teaching material

Introduction

- The Holy Spirit has remained masked and misunderstood for too long.
- In spite of what many people think he is not a ghost, he is the third person of the Trinity of God – Father, Son and Holy Spirit.
- It is easier for us to picture a Father, or Jesus the Son, so today we want to ask, 'Who is the Holy Spirit?'
- To do this we are going to take a quick tour through the Bible, starting at the very beginning . . .

1. He was involved in creation

Video clip – a clip that shows the grandeur and the beauty of creation:
  Contact: 00:00–06:00 amazing opening sequence to this film starring Jodie Foster, as a camera speeds through the entire cosmos
- The Holy Spirit is known as the breath of God.
- He was involved in the creation of the universe (Genesis 1:2).
- He breathed life into humans (Genesis 2:7).

2. Particular people, particular times, particular tasks

Illustration

Have somebody, or a number of volunteers, demonstrate a video game where the hero's energy supplies fade away as they fail. Note ways that the hero gained extra power, but note that it always wears off in the end. (If you want to go for that cool 'retro' feel, why not use PacMan?)

- In the Old Testament the Holy Spirit gave people power:
  - to express themselves in art: Bezalel (Exodus 31:1–5)
  - to lead: Gideon (Judges 6:14–16,34)
  - to perform feats of great strength: Samson (Judges 15:14–15)
  - to prophesy: Isaiah (61:1–3)

3. The Holy Spirit was promised by the Father

- God promised that at the right time the Holy Spirit would come in a new way (Ezekiel 36:26–27).
- The Holy Spirit would not just be on some people, some of the time, but on the inside of all believers all of the time (Joel 2:28–29).

4. Jesus and the Holy Spirit

- Around the time of Jesus the Holy Spirit became very busy.
- John the Baptist announced that someone was coming who would baptise people with the Holy Spirit (Luke 3:16).
- At Jesus' baptism the Holy Spirit came down on him and he received power (Luke 3:22, 4:1).
- Jesus predicted that his disciples would receive the Holy Spirit, but still they had to wait (John 7:37–39).

Conclusion

Video clip – *The Visual Bible*: Acts 2

- After Jesus' death, resurrection and ascension into heaven the Holy Spirit finally arrived.

- On the day of Pentecost the disciples were filled with the Holy Spirit in a completely new way.

- The disciples spoke in new languages, received new boldness and new power.

- Today the Holy Spirit is available to all of us. He can breathe new life into us, and give us power to live for God (Acts 2:38–39).

Weekend away: Talk 2 – What Does the Holy Spirit Do?

Teaching material

Introduction

- Like it or loathe it, we were all born into some kind of a human family.
- Just as we are physically born into a human family, so the Holy Spirit gives us a new birth into God's family (John 3:5–7).

1. Sons and daughters of God

- As Christians we have forgiveness for all that we have done wrong (Romans 8:1–2).
- The Spirit helps us to be sure that we are God's children (Romans 8:14–17).

2. Getting to know God better

Video clip – sometimes we all need help to understand:
> *Zorro*: the scene where a calm and collected Anthony Hopkins teaches a bumbling and aggressive Antonio Banderas how to sword fight.

- The Holy Spirit is able to help us understand God. The Holy Spirit can explain the wonderful truths of our relationship with God in practical ways that make sense to us.
- The Holy Spirit helps us to pray (Romans 8:26).
- The Holy Spirit helps us to understand the Bible (Ephesians 1:17–18).

3. Growing in the family likeness

- The Holy Spirit helps us to become more like Jesus
  - in every part of our lives (Galatians 5:22–23)
  - in every way (2 Corinthians 3:17–18)

4. One big family

Video clip – we are all different but we are all needed and have a part to play:
> *Legally Blonde*: 20:00–22:00 the tutor group introduce themselves

- The same Holy Spirit lives inside of every Christian regardless of nationality, church, age, or location in the world.
- We are all one family and with the help of the Holy Spirit we can learn to work together (Ephesians 4:3–6).

5. Gifts for all the children

Video clip – everyone has a particular gift to offer to the team:
> *X-men*: 25:30–28:15 the X-men interviews for special gifts
> *Mission Impossible*: breaking into Langley – everyone doing a different job
> *Lord of the Rings*: choosing the fellowship in Rivendel

- Just like a human parent, God loves to give gifts to his children.
- God also knows that each of his children is different and so he gives different gifts to each child.
- The gifts that God gives are for us to use to help the rest of the family (1 Corinthians 12).

6. A growing family

- The Holy Spirit gives us the power to live for Jesus.
- The Holy Spirit gives us the courage to tell others so that they can join the family (Acts 1:8).

Conclusion

- Every Christian has the Holy Spirit living in them.
- Not every Christian is *filled* with the Holy Spirit.
- The Bible says, 'Be filled with the Spirit' (Ephesians 5:18–20).

Discussion in small groups

- Which of these words would best have described your view of the Holy Spirit if you had been asked before this weekend?
  Ghost – God – ghoul – spiritual presence – comforter – helper – myth – power
  Are there any other words you would have used?

- How do you feel about / what do you think about the Holy Spirit having heard this morning's talks?

- Out of the six activities of the Holy Spirit mentioned in the second talk, which are most important to you?

  1. The Holy Spirit assures us we are God's children.

  2. The Holy Spirit helps us to get to know God better.

  3. The Holy Spirit helps us grow to become more like Jesus.

  4. The Holy Spirit helps Christians live together as one family.

  5. The Holy Spirit has gifts for each of us to use to help others.

  6. The Holy Spirit helps to make the Christian family grow.

Optional Bible study – in small groups

Read: 1 Corinthians 12:1–11 Spiritual gifts

- Has anyone in the group heard of or had any experience of spiritual gifts?

- What gifts are listed in this passage? (vv.8–10) Take some time to talk through the various gifts listed.

- Are you excited by the idea of God giving people supernatural gifts?
  Why or why not?

- Why does God give these gifts to people? (v.7)

Note: in the adult Alpha course this is often the point where the gift of tongues is discussed at some length. This is for clarity, and to reassure the members of the group about what might take place in the next session. You might like to bear this in mind for your group.

Weekend away: Talk 3 – How Can I Be Filled with the Holy Spirit?

Introduction

- To be strong Christians we need to be filled with the Holy Spirit.

1. What happens when people experience the Holy Spirit?

- The Book of Acts is the story of the start of the Christian church and it is filled with amazing instances of people being filled with the Holy Spirit.

Video clip – something that can't be seen – but its effects certainly can!

> *Twister*: opening scene
>
> *The English Patient*: dust storm sequence – can't see the wind, only the dust

- Similarly, we can't see the Holy Spirit, but when he moves powerfully, like in these instances from the book of Acts, we can certainly see the effects.

  – At Pentecost the Holy Spirit filled the disciples for the first time and they felt his power (Acts 2:2–4).

  – In Samaria the Holy Spirit's work was so dramatic that the local magician tried to buy his power (Acts 8:14–17).

  – When Paul received the Holy Spirit he got his sight back (Acts 9:17–19).

  – In Ephesus the people were able to speak God's messages in a new way through the Spirit (Acts 19:1–6).

  – In the house of Cornelius the Roman

    ❏ everyone knew when the people received the Holy Spirit (Acts 10:44–45)

    ❏ everyone was freed to praise God (Acts 10:46)

    ❏ everyone was given a new language of praise (Acts 10:46)
    This new language is sometimes called the gift of tongues.

It is a special language for prayer.

We can use it to pray for ourselves, for others, and to worship God.

(1 Corinthians 14)

(If you did not do so during the small group discussion / Bible study that followed the last session, then this would be a good time to explain more about the gift of tongues.)

2. Can anything stop us being filled?

Video clip – someone learns that they are the only obstacle:

> *The Matrix*: 46:30–52:50 Neo learns the only limitations are in his mind
> *Good Will Hunting*: he is a genius but needs to accept it for himself and act accordingly

- God wants to fill all his children with his Holy Spirit, but sometimes we put up barriers that make it difficult for us to be filled.

- We doubt that God wants to give us such a good gift – but he does (Luke 11:9–10).

- We get scared – but God loves us and his gifts are good (Luke 11:11–13).

- We doubt that we're worthy of the gift – but God promises to give to any who ask him (Luke 11:13).

Conclusion

- It's not enough to talk about being filled with God's Holy Spirit.

- We also need to give God the chance to fill us.

For guidance on leading this time of ministry, refer to 'Ministry on Youth Alpha' in the Practical Skills section of this manual.

Session 7 – How Can I Resist Evil?

Arrival atmospherics

The environment for this session is intended to get the young people thinking about the contrast between good and evil, light and darkness. From your knowledge of the sensibilities of your group judge how far it is appropriate to go with this.

- Using displays: make one side of the room light and the other dark, then place pictures and images on the walls that follow the theme.

- Using video: play clips of films of TV programmes that clearly show good battling evil.

- Using computers: play a game that follows the theme of good battling evil.

- Cueing the small groups: place a selection of magazines and newspapers in each small group area. Try to have different types available – current affairs, fashion, celebrity gossip, music, teen titles. (If you have a number of groups and this could prove expensive, use photocopies of relevant bits.)

Introduction to the session

- Welcome to this (evening's) session.

- Today we are going to be looking at the subject of evil.

- That might not seem like an appropriate subject for a course like this, but evil is a reality in the world and in our lives. There is no point burying our heads in the sand. It is far better to look at how God can help us to resist evil.

Unpacking the box – in small groups

Using a large sheet of paper (from a flip-chart, for example) draw a line across the whole of the middle of the page. At one end of the line write 'totally good', at the other end write 'totally evil'. Explain that this line represents a graph or a scale, one end is total evil, the other total good, the middle represents things that are neutral.

- Each of you, take a look through some of these magazines and pick out articles, advertisements or features that you consider interesting.

- Now, as a group we are going to place the articles, advertisements or features on this graph according to where we feel they fall on the scale from totally evil to totally good.
  Items that would be of interest to discuss would include current news stories, portrayals of women or of sex in advertising, horoscopes, sex tips and talks, true-life stories, the kind of advice given in the problem pages. Try to ensure the group includes some of these features.
  Follow up the exercise with some of these questions.

- How can we judge when something is evil?

- Do different members of the group have different opinions on what is evil?

- Are there certain things we all agree on? Why do we agree on these areas but not on others?

Teaching material

Introduction

- Christians believe that just as God is the source of all that is good and beautiful so the Devil is behind all evil and horror.

1. Why should we believe in the Devil?

Video clip – any film that portrays the Devil in a caricatured and unbelievable way: *Bedazzled*: 12:00–13:30 Liz Hurley introduces herself as the Devil

- Some young people find it easy to believe in the Devil, perhaps because of evil they have experienced or seen.

- Others find it almost impossible, perhaps because they are thinking of old wives tales and a devil with horns, pointed tail and a big fork, or of the Devil as portrayed in comedies.

- There are good reasons to believe in the Devil

  – because the Bible speaks of him

    in the Old Testament (Job 1; 1 Chronicles 21:1; Isaiah 14)
    in the New Testament (Ephesians 6:11–12; Luke 10:17–20)

  – because Christians have believed in him down the ages

  – because it is clear from the horror and evil in our world that he is at work

- BUT – it is just as dangerous to take too much of an interest in the Devil as to doubt that he even exists (Deuteronomy 18:10).

2. What does the Devil have to do with me?

- 'What on earth has the Devil go to do with me?' you might ask. 'Why would the Devil have any interest in me?'

- We know that the Devil aims to destroy all humans (John 10:10).

- The best way for him to do that is to try to keep us apart from God.
  He tries to blind our eyes so that we cannot see God (2 Corinthians 4:4).
  He tries to feed doubts into our minds (Genesis 3; Matthew 4:3,6).
  He tries to tempt us to do wrong (Genesis 3:6).

3. Should I be worried?

Video clip – hero protected by strong force of hidden friends so attackers turn tail and run:
Braveheart: 59:10–59:57

- It's quite natural that the thought that the Devil is out to get you might send a little shiver down your spine. But we have nothing to fear from the Devil.

- We have nothing to fear because
  Jesus has won a complete victory over the Devil (Colossians 2:15)

  as Christians we live in Jesus' kingdom not the Devil's kingdom (Colossians 1:13)

in Jesus' kingdom

there is:	forgiveness	instead of	sin
	freedom	instead of	slavery
	life	instead of	death
	salvation	instead of	destruction

4. So how do we defend ourselves?

- The book of Ephesians in the New Testament describes the armour that God has given us:

  – the belt of truth – knowing Jesus' truth to counter the Devil's lies (Ephesians 6:14)

  – the breastplate of righteousness – believing Jesus can protect us from guilt (Ephesians 6:14)

  – the boots of the gospel of peace – if we are ready to speak about Jesus (Ephesians 6:15)

  – the shield of faith – being sure of God's promises (Ephesians 6:16)

  – the helmet of salvation – protecting our minds from doubts (Ephesians 6:17)

  – the sword of the Spirit – getting to know the Bible and attacking the Devil with its truth (Ephesians 6:17)

5. How do we attack?

- We are not limited to just defending ourselves. We can also attack!

  by praying – the Devil trembles when we pray (2 Corinthians 10:4)

  by action – we attack the Devil by doing the things that Jesus told us to do (Luke 7:22)

Conclusion

- The Devil is real and so is his influence in the world, but he is no match for God.

- We have no cause to fear the Devil because we are now in Jesus' kingdom.

- There is no reason for great interest in the Devil. Why worry about a loser? In any case who wants to show interest in a loser?

Discussion in small groups

- If somebody had mentioned the Devil to you yesterday, what would have sprung immediately into your mind?

- Has your view of the Devil changed because of this session?

- Do you believe there is power in magic/witchcraft/the occult? Do you think being involved in these areas has a positive or negative effect on someone's life? Do you know anyone who is active in these areas? How does it affect them?

- Why do you think the world is in such a mess?

This discussion could throw up some pastoral issues. The team will need to have decided beforehand how they will deal with young people that are concerned about past experiences of occult powers. In the group context it is important to make sure that everyone feels affirmed and safe, and confident that God is far greater than any power of evil. Often, it will be a good idea to end this session with some powerful Bible verse about our loving, powerful heavenly Father, and/or with some fun and humour.

Optional Bible study – in small groups

Ephesians 6:10–20 The armour of God

- What do verses 11 and 12 tell us about the kind of spiritual fight that Christians face?

- What do you think each piece of armour represents? What do you think we need to do to be sure that we have each piece protecting us?

Session 8 – Why and How Should I Tell Others?

Arrival atmospherics

The environment for this session is intended to get the young people thinking about contagion.

- Using displays: put up medical posters and words and phrases like – Infection; Danger; Risk of Contamination; Germ alert; Biohazard Zone.

- Using video: have a contagion disaster movie playing – like *Outbreak*.

- Using computers: check the internet for information on viruses – how they spread, what are the most virulent, what to do to avoid them, stories of the effects of famous viruses.

Introduction to the session

- Welcome to this (evening's) session.

- Today we are going to be looking at the spread not of a disease, but of something far more positive, the spread of the Christian faith throughout the world.

- It is quite clear that there is something highly infectious and contagious about the faith. After all it started with just a handful of believers huddled together in an insignificant city in the Middle East and yet today there are not just millions, but billions of believers spread around the whole of the world.

- We need to understand something about the method of transmission. How is the Christian faith passed on?

Unpacking the box – in small groups

- Today we are going to imagine that we are a highly paid, highly skilled creative team at a top advertising agency.

- The day's challenge is to provide a top-drawer, rip-snorting campaign for one of our biggest clients.

- We need to sell Christianity.

- Think: What are the chief selling points that we can base our campaign on?
  What might our logo be?
  What slogans can we use to catch people's attention?
  What would the posters look like?
  What could we do for radio and television slots?

Depending on the wishes of your group you could just talk about this or you could provide the materials for some creative work (pens, pencils, paper) or even a computer with some design/desk top publishing software.

Teaching material

Introduction

Video clip – characters have some really, really good news they can't stop from sharing:
Dances with Wolves: when John Dunbar hears the buffalo and rides to the Latoka village in the middle of the night to tell them

- News – if it is really, really good it just can't be kept to yourself. You have to tell.

- Jesus also commanded his disciples to tell others (Matthew 28:16–20).

- It is not fair to keep to ourselves something that is needed by everyone.

- Although we were just thinking about advertising campaigns, the normal way for Christianity to be transmitted is for it to be passed from person to person. We all have a part to play in telling others.

- Right from the start it is good to recognise two possible mistakes:
  some go the religious fanatic route and force their views down other people's throats;
  some go silent and never let anyone know about their faith

- The key to avoiding these two mistakes is to

really care about the person you are telling and to trust God.

1. Live the message

- When people know that we are Christians they will watch how we live – our actions should match our words.

- In particular we should be careful to always treat other people well. To be a Christian, a follower of Jesus, is to follow his example and put others first (Matthew 5:13–16).

2. Talk the message

- It is likely that if we live like Christians people will want us to talk about it.

- When we talk about what we believe, people will ask questions. What about science – doesn't that disprove Christianity? What about suffering? What about other religions?

- We should be ready to answer.
  We don't all need to be theologians but we do need to be prepared for the questions that we might be asked. Reading the Bible is essential and there are other books to help us explain our faith (2 Corinthians 5:11).

This would be a good moment to recommend some books that you think might be appropriate for your group. (Nicky Gumbel, *Searching Issues*, Kingsway)

3. Present the message

Video clip – of a great preacher, or, for laughs, a caricature of a great preacher:

> *A Knight's Tale*: 33:00–36:00 the herald 'preaches' Sir Ulrich's praise (alternatively, you could video a clip of a preacher from a cable or satellite Christian TV channel)

- Fortunately we do not all have to be great preachers.

- We are all called to be witnesses. A witness is someone who tells of what they have seen or experienced. Just tell people what you have experienced of God.

- It can also be effective to take friends to hear the truth presented by someone or by a group who are especially good at explaining the faith (John 1:39–42).

4. Empower (the message)

Video clip – Acts 3 in *The Visual Bible*

- In the New Testament God used miracles to back up the message (Acts 3).

- God still does miracles today and we shouldn't be afraid to ask him to show his power to people.

5. Pray the message

- Prayer is essential:
  - pray that peoples' eyes would be opened to see the truth about God (2 Corinthians 4:4)
  - pray that God would give us boldness to talk about our faith (Acts 4:29–31)

Conclusion

- Never give up

- We might never know the effect of something that we have said or done, but God will use our lives and our words if we trust him (Romans 1:16)

Discussion in small groups

- If you did not know anything at all about Christianity how would you like to find out about it?

- If somebody was going to tell you about it what would be the best thing they could say?

- Do your family or your school friends know you come here/to church? What do they think about it?

- How do you feel about the idea of telling others?

Optional Bible study – in small groups

John 4:1–26 Jesus talks with a Samaritan woman

- What does the story tell us about the woman?

- How did Jesus make contact with her?

- What illustration did Jesus use? Why did he choose this image at this time? (vv.10, 13–14)

- What can we do to try to be relevant to our friends' interests and needs if we talk to them about Christianity?

Session 9 – Does God Heal Today?

Arrival atmospherics

The environment for this session is intended to get the young people thinking about the relationship (sometimes it seems to be a conflict) between faith and science.

- Using displays: put up scientific symbols, equations, diagrams and also Bible verses that speak of God's power and his miraculous involvement in the world.

- Using video: play a video such as *Leap of Faith* where an unexpected and genuine healing occurs.

- Using computers: have the group search for Christian testimonies of people who have been healed.

- Cueing the small groups: on each small group table/area have a collection of photocopied testimonies of healing.

Introduction to the session

- Welcome to this (evening's) session.

- In this session we are going to be looking at the subject of healing.

- We will be looking at whether God heals today.

Unpacking the box – in small groups

- Let's take a look at the articles that we have here.

We have provided a number of testimonies for you. If there is someone known to your group who has a testimony of healing, write up their story in a similar format and include it among the articles for the small groups.

- Do you find these stories believable? Why or why not?

- Do you believe that the stories you have just read are miracles of healing?

- Have any of you ever experienced anything miraculous?

Teaching material

Introduction

Video clip – the changing nature of faith and belief: *Captain Corelli's Mandolin*: 2:00–4:00 a healing takes place in the church procession but is it real?

- We are now living the first years of the 21st Century.

- The last century was perhaps the century of science. Many people believed that nothing that could not be readily explained by science could possibly occur. People tried to write the miracles out of the Bible and to argue that they were just invented fairy tales.

- Today people recognise the mystery of the world around, and are willing to admit that perhaps science can't give us all the answers, especially not to the most important and fundamental questions of life.

- This session is an explanation of why Christians, as well as rejoicing in the gift of medical science, also pray to God for miraculous healings.

- This session might also be the chance to pray for or to receive a miraculous healing.

1. Healing in the Bible

Video clip – Jesus performs a miracle of healing.

- Healing has always been a part of Christians' understanding of how God acts.

- Old Testament: God promises to heal (Exodus 23:25–26; Psalm 41:3). God said it was part of his character to heal (Exodus 15:26). There are examples of God healing (2 Kings 5; Isaiah 38–39).

- New Testament: The example of Jesus – 25 per cent of the Gospels are about healing.

The teaching of Jesus – healing as sign of the kingdom (Mark 1:14).

The kingdom of God is a key to understanding our experience of healing in the world today. The kingdom of God is both 'now' and 'not yet'. That means that when Jesus came he brought the kingdom of God. The healings that he did were some of the signs that the kingdom of God had arrived. But it hadn't arrived in its completeness. That will only happen when Jesus comes again. In the meantime, now, we live in the in-between times – the kingdom is here, but not completely here. When healings occur we see signs that the kingdom of God is here. Where healing doesn't happen we are reminded that we have to wait to see the kingdom come fully. (See Photocopy Sheet 15.)

Jesus sent his disciples out to pray for healing. (The 12 – Matthew 9:35–10:8; the 72 – Luke 10:1–20) Jesus also sends us out to heal in his name. (Matthew 28:16–20, Mark 16:15–20; John 14:9–14)

2. Healing in history

- There have been examples of healing and miracles throughout the history of the Christian church (Acts 3:1–10; Acts 5:12–16).

- In our small groups earlier we looked at some recent healings.
  (Re-examine some of these if you feel it would be of benefit to the group.)

3. How do we pray for healing?

Video clip – Alpha video healing session.
This point is most relevant if you are going to have a practical workshop on praying for each other. If you are not going to do so you should cut this down greatly. (See advice from 'Five Principles section' on p.40–1.) You should also consult the Ministry part of the Practical Skills section.

- Jesus healed people because he loved them (Mark 1:41; Matthew 9:36).

- It is important that we care and want the best for anyone we pray for.

- Prayers for healing should be simple, not long and complicated.

- The Holy Spirit might guide us in how to pray

– with a picture in our minds

– with a sympathy pain

– with a strong feeling

– with words in our minds

– with words for us to speak

- When we pray we should

  – ask where it hurts, how long it has hurt, and why it hurts

  – pray: that God would heal in the name of Jesus

  – ask: that the Holy Spirit would heal the person

  – continue: to be open to more guidance from the Holy Spirit

- Afterwards we should

  – ask the person how they feel

  – make sure that they are happy and understand all that has happened

Conclusion

- God does heal but not every person and not every time.

- Doctors don't have a 100 per cent success rate, but they don't stop being doctors and they don't stop trying.

- If we never pray for anyone then nobody will ever be healed.

Discussion and prayer – in small groups

Ask everyone for their reaction to the time of actually praying for healing that has followed the talk. It is important that everyone feels able to talk about what they are thinking and feeling even if it is negative or if they still have questions.

Ask if there is anyone who would like to be prayed for in the group. It could be a physical problem or any other matter. Pray for them according to the guidelines in the Ministry section of the Practical Skills section of this manual.

Make sure that everyone feels confident and accepted whether or not they chose to be involved in praying / being prayed for.

Session 10 – What about the Church?

Arrival atmospherics

The environment for this session is intended to get the young people thinking about belonging.

- Using displays: put up designs, posters, photos that speak of teams and belonging. They could be recognisable team strips and colours, family images, flags, fashion styles.

- Using video: either genuine team sports action or the exciting conclusion of team movie.

- Using computers: any video games that involve playing as a team.

- Cueing the small groups: give each of the small group areas a theme of belonging. One could be a sports team (do you have any of the bibs that are used to separate two teams, or is there a church or club sports strip?). Another could be a family. Another could be a particular youth social group. How about skaters with their distinctive clothing and activities? Another group could have a national identity. If you are willing to raise some difficult issues, how about a group defined by their racial identity? Or a group defined by disability? Use your imagination if you have more groups.

Introduction to the session

- Welcome to this (evening's) session.

- We are looking at the church.

- This is the worldwide group to which all Christians belong.

- The question is 'What is the church?' Is it just another club? Just a type of building? Just somewhere to waste a couple of hours on a Sunday morning? Or is it much, much more?

Unpacking the box – in small groups

Take some time to talk about the kind of identity that has been given to your group.

- How does this group define itself?

- What are the signs of being part of this group?

- Would you be proud to be thought of as part of a group of this kind?

- What are the good points about being a member of such a group? What is the downside?

Once you have had this discussion about the 'fictional' group identity assigned to you, return to the questions and go through the same procedure thinking now of the church.

How does the church, or the church youth group, or this small group define itself?

Teaching material

Introduction

Video clip – plays upon some popular misconceptions about the church:

> *Mr Bean Goes to Church*
> *A Knight's Tale*: 19:00–23:00 Will rides into a church following the girl

- Many people think of church as being mind-numbingly boring and totally useless.
  It can often seem that what is important to the church is totally different to what is important to young people.

- Here are some actual views of young people on the streets.

In the week preceding this session try to get out onto the streets of your town with either a video camera or a sound recorder. Ask young people to explain what comes into their heads when you say the word 'church'. Chances are the majority will not be flattering. Play the recording back to your young people.

- That is what young people on the street think of church, it might be similar to your views. But what is the church really about?

1. The people of God

- The church is not a building – it is made up of people (1 Peter 2:9–10).

- It is so much more than a few old people meeting together in the morning before they give their false teeth a work out on the Sunday roast.

- All believers that have ever lived anywhere in the world at any time make up the universal church.

- Today the church is huge – 1,900,000,000 people, more than 34 per cent of the world's population.

- Baptism is the visible mark of being a member of the church.

2. The family of God

- God is our Father. Nobody chooses their human family and many Christians look around and feel the same way about the people they see alongside them in the church (Ephesians 2:14–18).

- In spite of our many differences (of interest, dress sense, culture, personality) Jesus prayed that we would all be unified (John 17:11).

- We are brothers and sisters and we relate to God and to one another in the church (1 John 4:19–5:1).

3. The body of Christ

Video clip – team working together, the moment when it all comes right:
> *Remember the Titans*: 46:00–49:00 from the huddle to 'game titans'

- It's a great feeling to be part of a team when things are going well, with everybody working together to do their part and make good things happen. The church is more than just a team. The different parts of the church, you and I, are so closely related that the Bible describes it as being like the different parts of a body (1 Corinthians 12:1–26).

- We are all one in the Holy Spirit, just as different parts make up one body (Ephesians 4:3–6).

- We all have different gifts from God, just as different parts of the body have different roles.

- We all need each other, just as the different body parts need each other.

4. A holy temple

- A temple made of people – us (Ephesians 2:19–22).

- Built on the foundation of the apostles and prophets in the New Testament.

- With Jesus as the most important part – called the cornerstone.

- The Holy Spirit lives in this special temple.

5. The bride of Christ

Video clip – of a beautiful, desirable bride:
> *Runaway Bride*: 1:29:00–1:33:00 Julia Roberts runs, Richard Gere chases until she escapes on the FEDEX truck

- Jesus loves his church like a groom loves his bride (Ephesians 5:25–27, 32).

- We, the church, should respond to Jesus by living holy lives, worshipping him, and telling others about him.

Conclusion

- The church is about people: people in relationship to Jesus; people working together; people looking after one another; people serving and sharing good news with others.

Discussion in small groups

As this is the final week of Youth Alpha it is a good idea to have a general discussion of people's experiences, and what they have learned over the ten weeks. It is also worth talking about the future – do you have plans for the young people finishing Youth Alpha? Finally, try to finish by praying together.

- Can you summarise your experience on Youth Alpha? (Try to start with one of the most enthusiastic members of the group.)

- Has your view of the church changed over the last few weeks?

- Do you think you are going to continue involvement with this group and with the church?

- Should we set up a time for a social get together of this small group?

- Is there anything that you would like prayer for?

Weekend away: Talk 4 – How Can I Make the Most of the Rest of My Life?

Introduction

Video clip – someone gets a second chance at life:

> *Groundhog Day*: 55:00–1:01:00 Bill Murray replays one day over and over

- Unlike in that film we get no mocks, trials or practice runs at life, and perhaps that's a good thing – but how can we be sure of making the most of it?

- Read: Romans 12:1–21

1. What should we do?

- Make a break with the past – don't be squeezed into the mould that makes us just like everyone else.

- Make a new start – and let God transform us from the inside out (Romans 12:2).

2. How do we do it?

Video clip – working a transformation on someone:

> *Miss Congeniality*: 23:30–28:08
> *The Mask*: Jim Carrey character

- We must make a decision to offer every part of our lives to God and trust that he will help us to make the absolute best of our lives and ourselves (Romans 12:1).

  Our time – How do we use our time? How would God have us use it?

  Our ambitions – Are our goals God's goals for us?

  Our money – How do we use what we have? Selfishly or by giving?

  Our ears – Do we choose to listen to gossip, or believe the best about others?

  Our eyes – What do we chose to look at and watch – particularly on TV or in magazines?

  Our mouth/tongue – The tongue is very powerful. What do we say?

  Our hands – Do we give or do we take with our hands and skills?

  Our sexuality – God has made us sexual and he knows how best it can be a pleasure to us.

  Our masks – God wants us to take off our masks. We should recognise that if we live like this others might laugh at us, there might be suffering and sacrifice.

Conclusion – why we should do it

- Because God has a great plan for our future and this is the way to follow it (Romans 12:2).

- Because of all that God has done for us – we owe it to him (Romans 12:1 'in view of God's mercy').

ACTIVE STREAM
SESSION OUTLINES

General information

Arrival game[1]

These games are intended to ensure a live and exciting atmosphere for people to arrive into.

- No one should feel at a loss when they first turn up at the session.
- No one should be left standing alone in a corner of the room not knowing what to do.
- Whether they choose to throw themselves into the action by taking part, or simply join the crowd and watch the spectacle, everyone should feel involved.

The games have been chosen for their 'watchability' and also their 'flexibility' in involving as many people as wish to play for as long as is appropriate, and also because they are relatively easy to organise and do not require many props. Keep things moving, keep inviting (but not pressurising) newcomers to join in and you should find that your sessions start with laughter and a buzz.

The majority of the games would not work in somebody's front room, but neither do you need a sports field or a fully equipped gymnasium. If you can find a little bit of space – a garden, a hall, a classroom with chairs and tables pushed to one side – then you should be able to use these.

One game per session is provided but it may well be that after you have played two or three games the group find that they have a favourite which they want to play again. This is great – if they are having fun encourage them to play what they want. Alternatively, if the group really straggles in, you may find you need to play more than one game each week to keep things going. Never be afraid to put into action your own ideas if you can improve upon what is given.

There are one or two occasions where the arrival game is used as a link into the subject of these sessions, but these links are tenuous and you should easily be able to find a link of your own if you do not use the recommended game.

Introduction to the session

This is your moment (no more than a minute or two) to warmly welcome the young people, put them at their ease by giving them a glimpse of what will be happening through the session, and whet their appetite by mentioning the topic to be covered and hinting at why it might be of interest and import to them.

Getting to know one another – in small groups

On the adult Alpha course the small groups normally eat together at the start of the session. This gives an informal time to chat and get to know one another before the more directed discussion or Bible study later on.

Adults are generally well enough socialised to make small talk and then gradually progress into getting to know one another without too much help. The act of sharing a meal is normally enough to break down the barriers.

This is not necessarily the case with a group of young people, particularly not at the younger end of the 'youth' age range. It is also less likely that the sessions will be taking place at a natural time for a full meal. For these reasons we have added specific games or tasks into this section of the session. These are non-confrontational and help a group by providing simple tools for them to ask and answer questions about each other and gradually get to know one another. The kind of exercises and activities used progress throughout the course as it is assumed that the young people will be getting to know one another better and becoming more and more comfortable.

This is also a great time to share food. Depending on the timing of your course, the likes and dislikes of your participants, and the facilities available to you, the food could range from a full meal with multiple courses and proper cutlery, through finger-foods like pizza, burgers and hot dogs, down to a few crisps and sweets (fruits

---

[1] We would like to acknowledge the use of two books for some of the ideas in 'Arrival games' and 'Getting to know one another – in small groups': *Spectacular Stinking Rolling Magazine Book*, Pip Wilson (Marshall Pickering, 1991) and *Serendipity: Youth Ministry Resource Book*, Lyman Coleman (Scripture Union, 1989).

and vegetables if you are health conscious) to pick at as you chat.

Teaching material

The adult Alpha course, based on Nicky Gumbel's book *Alpha - Questions of Life*, is a wide ranging and in-depth introduction to the Christian faith. There is simply more material than is possible to present to a group of young people in an equivalent number of sessions, especially if those young people have not had previous exposure to Christianity, or if they are not used to book culture and abstract thinking.

For the course to work with youth the material must be reduced and simplified, without succumbing to the temptation to be simplistic, distorting the truth in an attempt to make it easier to understand.

The teaching outlines given here are not intended to substitute for your personal knowledge of the Alpha course material. They are intended to give you ideas on how to present the material and to reduce your preparation time. There will generally be more information provided than would be appropriate for one session. The idea is that you can contract the content (or expand points of particular relevance to your group), making use of your knowledge of the material and your understanding of your young people.

Throughout the outlines bullet points indicate what it is suggested the leader actually say – in your own words of course.

Activity – in small groups

These activities are designed for young people that are not yet comfortable with an open discussion of an abstract Christian principle, or who are not yet familiar enough or interested enough for a typical Bible study.

Note: discussion questions and Bible studies are available in this manual throughout the Alpha Tech stream. Please use these if you feel your groups will benefit from them. Perhaps these would be appropriate during the latter stages of the course.

Stream specific responsibilities to delegate:

- Arrival game organiser – to prepare for the game and lead it.
- Visual aid organiser – to obtain all that is needed and prepare for the presentations.
- Photocopy clerk – to photocopy correct numbers of worksheets.

Introductory session –
Is There More to Life than This?

Introduction

- If I were to mention Christianity to you, you might say: 'I'm young and this is the start of the 21st Century! What on earth does Christianity have to offer me?'

- On the face of it, the answer might be 'not much'.

   After all – many people consider Christianity and everything related to it to be boring

   many people are certain that the central claims of Christianity are untrue

   many people think that Christianity is irrelevant to life in the 21st Century

- BUT Jesus says, 'I am the way, the truth and the life' (John 14:6).

- I want to encourage you to take a look for yourself.

1. Direction

Project some optical illusions for the group to look at, and ask them questions related to what they see (or what they think they see).

- Things are not always as they first appear. The truth is sometimes hidden.

- Many people consider Christianity and everything related to it to be boring . . .

- BUT Jesus said 'I am the way'.

- Jesus/Christianity points the way to a life full of purpose and meaning – and fun.

2. Reality

Read the story of 'Pepe Rodrigues':
Pepe Rodrigues, one of the most notorious bank robbers in the early settling of the west of America, lived just across the border in Mexico. He regularly crept into Texas towns to rob banks, returning to Mexico before the Texas Rangers could catch him.

   The frustrated lawmen were so embarrassed by this

that they illegally crossed the border into Mexico. Eventually, they cornered Pepe in a Mexican bar that he frequented. Unfortunately, Pepe couldn't speak any English, so the lawmen asked the bartender to translate for them.

   The bartender explained to Pepe who these men were, and Pepe began to shake with fear. The Texas Rangers, with their guns drawn, told the bartender to ask Pepe where he had hidden all the money he had stolen from the Texas banks. 'Tell him that if he doesn't tell us where the money is right now, we're going to shoot him dead on the spot!'

   The bartender translated all this for Pepe. Immediately, Pepe explained in Spanish that the money was hidden in the town well. They could find the money by counting down 17 stones from the handle and behind the 17th stone was the loot he'd stolen.

   The bartender then turned to the Rangers and said in English, 'Pepe is a very brave man. He says that you are a bunch of stinking pigs, and he is not afraid to die!'

   (Adapted from *Hot Illustrations*, Wayne Rice, 1994, Youth Specialties)

- Things sometimes get lost in translation. If much of what you know about Christianity is second-hand information, you owe it to yourself to check it out properly – yourself.

- Many people consider that the central claims of Christianity are untrue.

- BUT Jesus said, 'I am the truth'.

- With Jesus/Christianity to show us the truth we can make sense of the crazy, mixed-up world around us.

3. Life

- It's dark out there.

- The world can be a dark place and the line between darkness and light passes through the heart of each of us.

- Every one of us has the potential to do good or evil with our lives.

- Many people think that Christianity is irrelevant to life in the 21st Century.

- BUT Jesus said, 'I am the life'.

- With Jesus we can turn our backs on evil and live forever in the light.

Conclusion

- Christianity is not boring – it is about living life to the full.

- Christianity is not untrue – it is the truth.

- Christianity is not irrelevant – it transforms the whole of our lives.

- REMEMBER – things are not always as they first appear
  if much of what you know about Christianity is second-hand information, that may or may not be true

- You should check it out for yourself.

Session 1 – Who Is Jesus?

Arrival game

Place players in two lines.

Hand a water balloon to the first person in each line. These balloons must be passed backwards as fast as possible, over the shoulder of the first person, then under the legs of the second, over the shoulder of the third, and so on to the back of the line. When the balloon reaches the last person he or she runs to the front of the line and restarts the process. The relay is finished when the first person returns to the front of the line.

Feed spare water balloons into the relays wherever they burst.

More balloons per line / more water per balloon = more wetness!

Introduction to the session

As this is the first session take slightly longer over your introduction. Introduce Youth Alpha and explain a little of what will be happening throughout the course. Think of it as a bus journey. The group don't need to know the name of every street they pass, but they need to know the general direction they are going in!

- Welcome the group.
- Introduce the Alpha course.
- Explain that we all choose to follow someone – a sports star, a big brother, a fashion icon.
- Who is it that Christians follow? And why?

Getting to know one another – in small groups

For the first session a very simple information exchange is made slightly more dynamic by the addition of low flying objects.

With the group standing or seated in a circle start with names. The first person holds a ball or other similarly aerodynamic and non-sharp-edged object and gives their name. They then throw the object to another person across the circle, who catches it (normally),

gives their name, and then throws it to the next person. Once everyone has given their name, they must add another fact about themselves. Go on adding new facts as long as memory and interest permits. The repetition should mean that at least the names get well ingrained.

You could test the group by reversing the order at the end of play so that you have to give the information relating to the person who threw the ball to you.

Teaching material

Introduction

As an opening illustration, ask one of the young people to take a coin out of their pocket, wallet or purse. Ask when it was made. Then: 1996 (for example), that's one thousand nine hundred and ninety-six years since what? The answer is 1996 years since the birth of Jesus Christ, so . . .

- 'Who is Jesus?'
- The old Communist dictionary used to say that Jesus was a 'mythical figure who never existed'. That means that he was made up/invented by other people.
- We now know that is not the case – we know that Jesus existed and most people agree these facts about him:

  a Jewish man who was born in Bethlehem in Judaea around 4 BC.
  famous as a great teacher and miracle worker.
  crucified by the Roman authorities.
  his followers believed he was the Son of God and that he rose from the dead, and they took the good news through the world.

- The New Testament of the Bible is our best source of information about who Jesus is. Don't worry if you don't know much about the Bible or why you should have any confidence in it. We will look at the Bible in more detail in a later session. You just need to know that for Christians it is a holy book, and that it tells us a great deal about Jesus.

1. Jesus was fully human

- Jesus was clearly human, with a body, emotions, and experiences like ours (John 4:6; Matthew 4:2; Mark 11:15–17; John 11:32–36; Mark 6:3; Luke 2:46–52).
  The question that we must ask today is: Was Jesus more than human? Was he God?

2. What did he say about himself?

Read the story from the box below:
Imagine a new teacher arriving at a school. The school is failing – an educational disaster area. Unlike the rest of the zombies and wannabe-dictators the school employs, this new man is dynamic. He's interesting, he's brilliant and he cares about you, the students, not just about results, the girls fancy him and in time the boys start talking and dressing like him. In short, he's the best thing that's happened to the school since they started serving chips in the cafeteria.

Then it happens. In the middle of Wednesday morning assembly he gets to his feet and announces: 'I am the bread of life. Whoever comes to me will never go hungry.' There's a stunned silence. Ms Frittle, the tone deaf music mistress who has a bit of a thing for the new teacher, is so shocked that her mouth drops open and her false teeth fall out.

The new teacher hasn't finished though. Turning to Form 10C, the biggest bunch of delinquents in the school, he declares: 'I am the light of the world. Whoever follows me will never walk in darkness.' The headmaster's notes drop to the floor with a crash and the first of many giggles ripple around the room.

Still the new teacher is not finished. 'I am the resurrection and the life. He who believes in me will live even though he dies; and he who lives and believes in me will never die.' By now the school secretary is on the phone to the nearest mental hospital and the head of Year 7 is quietly ushering the petrified 11 and 12 year-olds out of the fire exit.

Unconcerned, the new teacher turns to where the PE teachers are seated. 'Your sins are forgiven,' he says. (Jonathan Brant, *My Whole World Jumped*, Kingsway 2002)

- That is not too different from what happened to Jesus' followers 2000 years ago.
  Their wonderful, wise teacher also made outrageous claims about himself.
  I am the bread of life (John 6:35)
  I am the light of the world (John 8:12)
  I am the resurrection and the life (John 11:25–26)
  I am the way, the truth and the life (John 14:6)

- Jesus didn't make it possible for us to think of him as just a good man. A normal man who said the things Jesus did wouldn't be good at all. If he believed what he said he would have to be a madman. If he didn't believe it but said it anyway (just to get influence over people) then he would be a bad man, a con man.

- So why do we believe that Jesus was not a madman or a con man but the one and only God man?

3. What evidence is there?

- There is evidence for Jesus being more than just a man in:
  - his teaching (Matthew 5–7)
  - his works (John 10:37–38)
  - his character
  - his fulfilment of Old Testament prophecy
  - his resurrection from the dead

Conclusion

- Most fashions, fads and crazes come and go. (You might like to ask the young people to list some recent short lived fads and crazes.)

- But 2000 years after the death of Jesus, not millions but billions of people follow him. (You might like to give a short personal testimony of the reality of following Jesus.)

Activity – in small groups

- Conspiracy theories are nothing new.

- One piece of evidence for Jesus being more than just a good man is the fact that he rose from the dead. People who don't believe this have come up with some conspiracy theories of their own to explain why the body was missing from the tomb.

Hand out copies of photocopy sheet 1 to the group, or simply read them the different theories.

- Are any of these believable? Why or why not?

Make a list of the group's responses to the theories. Then work quickly through Photocopy Sheet 2 (p.107) adding the information given there to what you have already discussed.

- The miraculous resurrection of Jesus from the dead is very hard for humans to believe, so it is no wonder that people have tried to find other, less remarkable, explanations to fit the facts. However, none of these explanations stand up to careful consideration.
Christians believe that Jesus really was God and that he really was raised from the dead.

Photocopy Sheet 1 – The conspiracy theories

These facts are agreed by everybody; believer and sceptic alike.

Fact 1 – The Romans crucified Jesus.

Fact 2 – Jesus' body was placed in a tomb closed with a large stone and guarded by soldiers.

Fact 3 – On the third day after Jesus' death the tomb was found to be empty.

Fact 4 – The belief that Jesus had been raised from the dead spread through the known world.

Conspiracy Theory One – Jesus didn't really die

Some people have argued that Jesus didn't really die on the cross – he only passed out from the pain and exhaustion. They believe that when he was taken off the cross and laid down in a comfortable position in a cool tomb he simply recovered consciousness, got up and walked off into the sunset to live happily ever after.

Conspiracy Theory Two – The disciples stole the body

Some people believe that in the middle of the night the disciples crept up and overpowered the sleepy Roman guards. They then rolled the stone away from the entrance to the tomb, picked up Jesus' lifeless body and disappeared into the night. They started the rumours that Jesus had risen from the dead in order to make themselves seem more important. Throughout the rest of their lives they never let on to anyone what they had done.

Conspiracy Theory Three – The authorities secretly removed Jesus' body

Some people think that the Jewish and Roman authorities worked together to steal and get rid of Jesus' body, perhaps because they didn't want the tomb to become a kind of religious shrine or holy place constantly crowded with Jesus' old followers. So they simply took the body and buried it somewhere else, somewhere secret.

Photocopy Sheet 2 – Problems with the conspiracy theories

Conspiracy Theory One – Jesus didn't really die

Even before being hung on the cross Jesus was brutally beaten and tortured.

Roman soldiers, who knew when their victim was dead, carried out the crucifixion.

Dead bodies in those days were wrapped like mummies in cloth and sticky spices.

To escape the tomb Jesus would have had to get out of the grave clothes, roll away a heavy stone and fight the soldiers.

Conspiracy Theory Two – The disciples stole the body

The disciples were scared and confused; they weren't thinking of a daring rescue.

The disciples could not have overpowered the soldiers guarding the tomb.

It is believed that all the disciples were eventually killed for their belief in Jesus' resurrection. Surely at least one of them would have confessed the truth to save his skin?

Conspiracy Theory Three – The authorities secretly removed Jesus' body

The authorities hated the fast spreading belief that Jesus was alive and had risen from the dead.

If they had had the body, or known where it was, they would simply have produced it and thrown it down in a public place to prove to everyone that Jesus really was dead.

They didn't do this, so we have to assume that they didn't have the body.

Conclusion

None of these theories are very believable.

Also, none of them can account for the fact that over 500 people are reported to have seen Jesus alive in the weeks following his crucifixion.

Session 2 – Why Did Jesus Die?

Arrival game

Swing-ball elimination

To build your swing-ball simply tie a length of thick string or thin rope to the handles of a bag filled with a large, light ball (volleyball, football), or a cushion, or some scrunched up clothes – anything relatively soft but with a bit of weight.

The game is simplicity itself. The players stand in a circle around the central person holding the swing-ball. The central player then starts to swing the swing-ball around and around keeping it roughly level and less than 40 cm off the ground. At the command 'Go!' all the players must step in within the radius of the swing-ball circle and start jumping over it as it swings around. If a player is touched they must retire and the game progresses until a single winner is left.

Introduction to the session

- Welcome the group.
- Pose the question, 'Why did the chicken cross the road?' and judge the best answers.
- Make the point that 'Why?' is a very important question.
- Today's 'Why?' is 'Why did Jesus die?'

Getting to know one another – in small groups

Arrange the chairs for the group in two circles – one inside the other. The inner circle of chairs faces outwards and the outer circle inwards.

Read out the first question on the list below and allow each member of the pair (one person facing out from the inner circle together with the person facing in at them from the outer circle) one minute to answer the question.

When the two minutes are up the outer circle rotates by one place so that new pairs are formed. Read the next question.

Continue to rotate every two minutes until all the questions have been answered.

1. Where I go to school, and what I think of school.
2. My favourite TV programmes.
3. The greatest moment of my life so far.
4. The person I know best in this room.
5. How I came to be here today.
6. What I think of Youth Alpha so far.

Teaching material

Introduction

Copy and hand out, or copy onto acetate and project, photocopy sheet 3. Ask for people to comment upon the four very respectable looking ladies. Ask what is unusual about them. Is there an odd one out? If the students haven't caught it yet ask them to look closely at the jewellery being worn.

Lady one – hang man's noose earrings

Lady two – pearl necklace

Lady three – electric chair earrings

Lady four – cross around neck

- The odd one out is the lady with the pearls. Only she isn't wearing an instrument of death and torture as jewellery.
- Why is it that an instrument of torture and execution is the most common and recognisable symbol of the Christian faith? Why is the cross at the heart of the Christian faith? (1 Corinthians 2:2)

Rather than having one key teaching point, the illustration/visual aid for this session covers all the points of the talk. The tasks associated with the visual aid are interspersed with the main teaching points. You might wish to have a well-practised assistant actually perform the tasks while you talk the group through it.

You will need: a glass jug or other clear container
water
a plastic or wooden cross with a
container fixed to its bottom
iodine
hypo crystals
(the iodine and hypo crystals are
available from photographic shops)

1. The problem

- We humans have a problem – we have all done wrong. The Bible, and Christians who follow the Bible, call this sin.

- Sin is an old fashioned and unpopular word but it refers to all that we do wrong (Romans 3:23). (Take a moment to explain sin to your group in a manner that they will understand.)

- The problem with the things we do wrong is that they make us dirty on the inside. (Mark 7:21–23)

Place the empty container of clear water in front of the group.

- When God made humans he made them perfect and clean.

- But we all disobey God by doing wrong and that has dirtied us.

- List some kinds of sin that are appropriate to your group and drip some iodine onto the top of the water. Stir the water to show the iodine spreading throughout.

- The things that we do wrong keep us from God. God is so pure that he can't be near dirt produced by sin. (Perhaps, it's a bit like Superman and kryptonite.) Separated from God we will die, and not enjoy life after death.

2. The solution

- God knew that there was nothing we could do to make ourselves clean.
Make a show of stirring the water without success.

- But he loves us and wanted to be close to us again. He knew that he would have to be the one to take action.

- God's solution was the death of Jesus on the

cross. God gave himself to die for us (1 Peter 2:24).

- The death of Jesus on the cross had amazing results.

- Place the cross with the pouch of hypo crystals on the back of it into the water and begin to stir it round. The water will gradually clear until it is as clean as in the first instance.

3. The result

- It is a mystery exactly how it works, but the Bible teaches that the death of Jesus (who was sinless, who had never done wrong) makes a wonderful difference to us (Romans 3:21–26).

- Jesus' death on the cross takes away our sin and makes us clean again, unstained by all the wrong things we have done.

- Jesus' death on the cross means that God is no longer separated from us, and we can begin a relationship with him (2 Corinthians 5:19).

Conclusion

- God loves each of us and longs to be in relationship with us.

- If you had been the only person in the world Jesus would have died for you (Galatians 2:20).

- If we believe that Jesus suffered on the cross for us and if we say sorry for the things that we have done wrong (our sins), we can know God.

Small group activity

For the small group activity each group should work through the illustration used in the talk once more. As they are working, and as they do the illustration, use the readings and questions to reflect with them on the teaching of the session.

Step One: Make the cross with pouch or container attached

Provide the group with materials to cut out a cross and attach a container/pouch. (For example, cardboard for the cross, and a bottle top to tape on the back of it that they can later put the hypo crystals in.)

Read the description of the crucifixion below:

Cicero described crucifixion as 'the most cruel and hideous of tortures'. Jesus was stripped and tied to a whipping post. He was flogged with four or five thongs of leather interwoven with sharp jagged bone and lead. Eusebius, the third-century church historian, described Roman flogging in these terms: the sufferer's 'veins were laid bare, and . . . the very muscles, sinews and bowels of the victim were open to exposure'. He was then taken to the Praetorium where a crown of thorns was thrust upon his head. He was mocked by a battalion of about 600 men and hit about the face and head. He was then forced to carry a heavy cross bar on his bleeding shoulders until he collapsed, and Simon of Cyrene was press-ganged into carrying it for him.

When they reached the site of crucifixion, he was again stripped naked. He was laid on the cross, and six-inch nails were driven into his forearms, just above the wrist. His knees were twisted sideways so that the ankles could be nailed between the tibia and the Achilles' tendon. He was then lifted up on the cross which was then dropped into a socket in the ground. There he was left to hang in intense heat and unbearable thirst, exposed to the ridicule of the crowd. He hung there in unthinkable pain for six hours while his life slowly drained away.

Yet the worst part of his suffering was not the physical trauma or torture and crucifixion nor even the emotional pain of being rejected by the world and deserted by his friends, but the spiritual agony of being cut off from his father for us – as he carried our sins. (Nicky Gumbel, *Alpha - Questions of Life*, Kingsway, p.44–5)

Ask: How do you feel about what Jesus suffered?

Step Two: Place the iodine in the previously clear water

Provide a glass or other container full of clean water and the iodine.
The group adds the iodine as it was done during the talk.
Explore the group's understanding of sin.
Can they recognise sin in their lives? Do they ever feel guilty for things they do wrong? Do they ever feel unclean?

Step Three: Add the cross with the hypo crystals in the container

When the group has performed this stage in the illustration . . .
Ask: Does it seem like magic that the iodine disappears?
We know that it is a chemical reaction but we can't explain it.
Do you think it matters that we can't exactly explain how it is that Jesus' death on the cross makes us clean and allows us to have a relationship with God?

Note: the leaders might like to have in their minds the four different images/illustrations used in *Alpha - Questions of Life* Chapter 3 to describe the results of Jesus' death on the cross.

Photocopy Sheet 3 – Ladies with jewellery

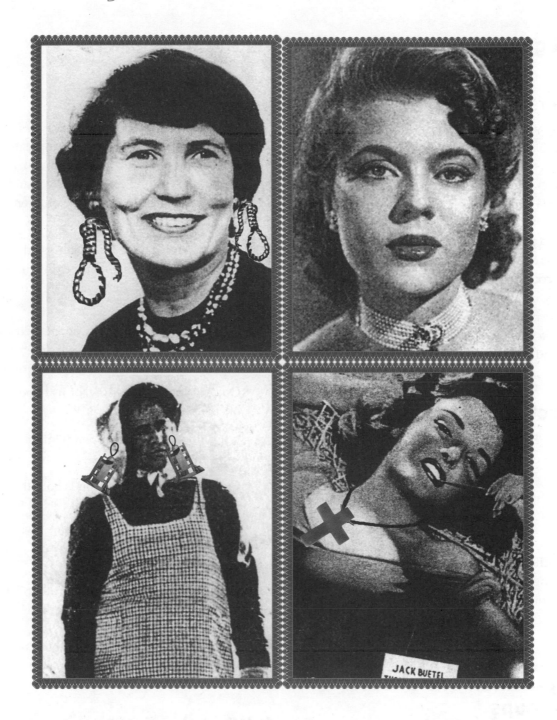

Who is the odd one out?

Session 3 – How Can We Have Faith?

Arrival game

Banana relay

Divide those young people that wish to play into two teams. Each team then divides down into pairs.
Set out a course to be run. Eg using chairs or cones or other markers.
Give a banana to each couple.
The first pair from each team must peel their banana, place one end in each of their mouths and then set off down the course. The object is to make their way around the course and back to their team without breaking the banana held in their mouths.
When they arrive back the next pair sets off and so on. If you break a banana you have to go back to the beginning and start again with a new one.

Introduction to the session

• Welcome the group.

Prepare a list of five facts about yourself.
Three of these facts should be true and two should be false. Give your five facts and have the group vote true or false for each one. At the end of each vote give the true answer.

• It is difficult to be completely sure about anything, isn't it? Nonetheless today we want to talk about how it is possible to be sure about our faith.

Getting to know one another – in small groups

In the small groups play a variation on the game the leader just played.
Members of the group must think of three facts to give about themselves – two should be true, one false.
Go around the group each person giving their three facts. The rest of the group must try to guess which fact is false.

Teaching material

Introduction

Lay out several glasses with different types of coke or cola in them. Make sure the young people do not see which bottle you pour into which cup. Ask a few volunteers to sample the cokes and colas and see if they can identify the flavours of the different brands by placing the correct bottle behind each cup.

• Even when we have tried and tasted things for ourselves it can sometimes be difficult to be sure exactly what we taste. Is it the 'real thing' or an imitation?

• Some people feel that way about their faith, about Christianity. We all have different experiences, so how can we be sure of our faith?

• God has made it possible for us to be sure about our faith (2 Corinthians 5:17).

Bring out a stool or camera tripod with the legs removed/contracted.

• Christians believe that God is both three and one – one God but three persons.

• It's a brain breaker but the name given is the Trinity. (If you have time you could give an illustration of Trinity.)

• Each member of the Trinity – Father, Son and Holy Spirit – has a part to play in helping us to be sure of our faith.
It is as if each one of them supplies one leg of this stool/tripod.

1. What the Father promises

• It is safer to rely on God's promises in the Bible than on our changeable feelings.
God promises that he will come in to our lives if we ask him (Revelation 3:20).
God promises that he will be with us forever (Matthew 28:20).
God promises to give us eternal life with him in heaven (John 10:28).

As you are speaking screw one of the legs into the stool, or extend it out of the tripod.

Ask for a volunteer to sit on the stool (without putting their feet down) or balance a glass of water on top of the tripod.

Ask: Are you sure you can do this? They won't be. (If you have a real dare-devil determined to give it a try make sure they don't hurt themselves. Broken back = law court!)

2. What Jesus did

- We can never earn God's forgiveness but Jesus died to destroy the barrier between God and us (John 3:16).
  (Look back to last week if this is a helpful moment for a review.)

- We take advantage of what Jesus has done for us through faith.

- To answer the question 'What is faith?' tell this story from the box below:
  John Patton was a Scot but he travelled all the way from Scotland to a group of islands in the South West Pacific to tell the tribal people about Jesus. The islanders were cannibals and his life was in constant danger. When he tried to translate the Bible into their language he found there was no word for 'belief' or 'trust'. Nobody trusted anybody else. Finally, he thought of a way to find the word he was looking for when one of the tribal people came in to his study. Patton raised both his feet off of the ground, leant back in his chair and asked the man, 'What am I doing now?' The servant gave him a word, which means 'to lean your whole weight upon'. This was the word Patton used in his translation of the Bible.
  (Nicky Gumbel, *Alpha - Questions of Life*, Kingsway, p.59)

Pick up the tripod or stool again and screw back in, or pull out the second of the legs.

Now, ask another volunteer to try sitting on the stool or balancing the glass of water on top of the tripod. Once again ask, 'Are you sure you can do this?'

- With only two legs we still can't have complete faith. Although we are much closer we can't yet 'lean our whole weight upon'. Happily there is a final reason we can be sure of our faith.

3. What the Spirit does

- When someone becomes a Christian God's Holy Spirit comes to live within them (Romans 8:9).

- The Holy Spirit inside of us changes us from the inside out (Galatians 5:22–23).

- He fills us with a certainty that God is our Father and that he loves us (Romans 8:15–16).

Put in place the final leg of the stool or tripod and again ask for a volunteer.

In answer to your asking 'Are you sure you can do this?' they should answer an emphatic 'Yes!'

Have them take a seat, or balance the glass and then give them a prize for doing so.

Conclusion

- I asked the last volunteer 'Are you sure?' and the answer was yes.

- We can be sure that our faith is true.

- This is not arrogant or proud because we are not trusting in ourselves. We are trusting in God: his promises to us; his work to free us from sin; and his Holy Spirit changing us from the inside out.

Activity – in small groups

Tripod building – small group competition

Hand out to the group ten drinking straws, a 30cm long piece of sticky tape and a pair of scissors. Each group must build the strongest possible tripod out of the materials they have been given in the time that you set – test the tripods by placing books on top of them. The strongest tripod is the winner.

Finish by discussing in the small groups how strong their relationship with God feels. Would their 'tripod' be one of the first to fail or do they feel that their faith can stand up to all the pressures and weights of life?

Show the swimming pool illustration from photocopy sheet 4.

Ask: Where do you feel you are in your relationship with God?

Where do you feel you are in your relationship with God?

Session 4 – Why and How Do I Pray?

Arrival game

Caterpillar Racing

Don't worry this won't have animal rights activists up in arms. The caterpillars are made up of young people – five to eight of them to be exact (and I'm afraid that girls wearing skirts should probably be excluded). The young people form the caterpillars by sitting down on the floor one immediately behind the other. Each person (except the one at the front obviously) wraps their legs around the waist of the person in front so that their feet are resting in that person's lap. They then place their hands on the shoulders of the person in front. Your caterpillars are now ready – let them race!

A few hints:

Only the player at the front may allow his feet to touch the ground.

Nobody can touch the ground with his or her hands. This shuffling along on your buttocks is very hard work – so be sure to make the course a short one!

Introduction to the session

- Welcome the group.
- Some of us probably have blisters in painful places as a result of those hard fought caterpillar races. The truth is, the human body just wasn't made to walk on its behind.
- Talking of unnatural positions, many of you probably associate prayer with boredom and cramp because of being forced to kneel as a child or in church.
- Today we are going to be looking at why prayer is one of the greatest privileges of life.

Getting to know one another – in small groups

Hand out pens and paper and explain to the group that they must each write a 'For Sale' advert for themselves. The adverts need to be short and punchy, as if they were to go in a newspaper classifieds section.

They must focus on the positives of what makes the writer so valuable a person.

Once the group have all written their adverts the leader should collect them in and then read them out one at a time.

Try to guess who wrote each advert.

Teaching material

Introduction

Have five volunteers leave the room and then call them back in, one at a time.

When they return explain to them that you are going to set the scene, give them a piece of information and then start a sentence for them – they must finish the sentence immediately with the first thing that comes into their head.

- You are in an examination.
- You've just turned over your paper and read the examination.
- You realise you don't know the answer to a single question.
- Finish this sentence:
- 'The first thing I would do is . . .'

As each volunteer gives his or her answer write it down on a big sheet of paper or on an OHP.

Prayer may or may not be mentioned by your volunteers but in either case make this point.

- In such a horrible situation many of us would pray. In fact surveys show that 75 per cent of the population admit to praying at least once a week – many of those wouldn't even consider themselves believers.
- So what is so special about prayer? Why and how do Christians pray?

1. What is prayer?

- Prayer should be exciting, and it should be the most important activity of life, because it is about relationship with the most powerful and most wonderful person in the universe (Matthew 6:5–13).

- Might ask, 'But can I really build a relationship with God through prayer? I won't really hear a voice or experience God speaking to me will I?'

Illustration exercise on non-verbal communication

For this exercise you will need to pick one simple sentence and then explore the different ways – of which speaking is only one – that it can be communicated:

- speaking it
- writing it
- drawing it with symbols
- drawing a picture
- actions
- sign language
- acting it out in a mime
- by touch

Have the group brainstorm different ways of communication like the ones given above and then see who can use these to communicate different relational sentences such as:

- I love you.
- I'm cross with you.
- You're funny.

When we think about relating to God in prayer we must be aware that God can speak to us in many different ways. We don't have to wait for an audible voice.

2. Why pray?

- Because prayer develops our relationship with God – friendship is about time spent together.

Voice recognition illustration

Have a volunteer join you at the front and stand with his back to the rest of the group. Explain that when you point at a member of the group they must call out 'Hello!' The volunteer must try to guess who called out.

- When a friend that we know well calls out, even just one word, we can recognise their voice. As

our relationship/friendship with Jesus grows we can learn to recognise him speaking to us.

- Because we are to copy Jesus – and he prayed a lot (Mark 1:35; Luke 6:12; 9:18,28; 11:1).
- Because it brings us joy and peace – even in difficult situations (John 16:24; Matthew 7:7–11).
- Because it changes situations – prayer works.

3. Does God always answer my prayer?

- We can let things create a barrier between us and God
  - if we are disobedient (1 John 3:21–22)
  - if we don't forgive (Matthew 6:14–15)
  - if we haven't told God about the things we've done wrong (Isaiah 59:2)
  - if our motives are wrong (James 4:2–3)
- Sometimes we want things that are not good for us – God will only give us what is best for us (Matthew 7:11).
- Remember that 'Yes', 'No' and 'Wait' are all answers.

4. How do we pray?

- To help us to pray we can follow a pattern:

  T   Thank you – praise God for all he has given you.

  S   Sorry – admit to God what you have done wrong.

  P   Please – ask God for what you and others need.

- You can pray any time and any place, while doing anything (1 Thessalonians 5:17).
  BUT . . . it is good to have a regular time when you can pray alone and not be distracted (Matthew 6:6), and times when you can learn to pray with other people (Matthew 18:19).

Small group activity

Hand out this text message prayer to the group: cut off of the top of photocopy sheet 7. Take time together to decipher it and translate it into to more common English.

dad@hvn, urspshl.we want wot u want@urth 2b like hvn.giv us food&4giv r sins lyk we 4giv uvaz.don't test us!save us!bcos we kno ur boss, ur tuf&ur cool 4 eva!ok?

Once they have made their translation ask if anybody recognises it.

It is the most famous prayer in the world, the Lord's Prayer that Jesus taught us.

Hand out the full photocopy sheet to the group.
Read Matthew 6:9–13 in the different translations.

Allow the group time to compose a text message prayer and enter their text onto a phone.
In a moment of quiet send each group's prayer to the leader's phone and have the leader read them out one by one.

Photocopy Sheet 5 – Prayer

dad@hvn, urspshl.we want wot u want@urth 2b like
hvn.giv us food&4giv r sins lyk we 4giv
uvaz.don't test us!save us!bcos we kno ur boss, ur
tuf&ur cool 4 eva!ok?

Matthew 6:9–13 The Message

Our Father in heaven,
Reveal who you are.
Set the world right;
Do what's best –
        as above, so below.
Keep us alive with three square meals.
Keep us forgiven with you and forgiving others.
Keeps us safe from ourselves and from the Devil.
You're in charge!
You can do anything you want!
You're ablaze in beauty!
        Yes. Yes. Yes.

Matthew 6:9–13 NIV

Our Father in heaven,
hallowed be your name,
your kingdom come,
your will be done on earth as it is in heaven.
Give us today our daily bread.
Forgive us our debts,
As we also have forgiven our debtors.
And lead us not into temptation,
But deliver us from the evil one.
For yours is the kingdom and the power and the glory
for ever.
Amen.

Session 5 – Why and How Should I Read the Bible?

Arrival game

'I'm all right, Jack!'

This is a card game, but it's not quite as sedate and decorous as your grandmother's bridge club. It involves action and is quite amusing to watch.

Sit the players in a circle and give the dealer a pack of playing cards. The dealer simply slaps the cards down, face up, in the centre of the circle while the rest of the group watch intently.

When the dealer turns up a Jack – the group must shout 'I'm all right, Jack!'

When the dealer turns up a Queen – the group must stand to their feet and curtsey.

When the dealer turns up a King – the group must stand to their feet and salute.

When the dealer turns up an Ace – the group must stand and move around to the next seat in the circle.

When the dealer turns up a seven – the group must do all of the above in the order listed.

Ideas: Play as an elimination game – last person to react is out.
Come up with your own actions – as wild as you like!

Introduction to the session

- Welcome the group.
- Read a love letter.
    or
- Read a funny e-mail.
- Written communication is very important, between lovers, friends, business partners.
- Today we are going to be looking at God's written communication to us – the Bible.

Getting to know one another – in small groups

Each member of the group has to complete these four sentences. They must complete three truthfully and one falsely.

If I could marry any famous person, I would marry . . .
If I had all the money in the world, I would drive . . .
If I could live in any part of the world, I would live in . . .
If I could have any job, I would be a . . .

Once the group have had a few minutes to work on their answers have each person read back their sentences while the rest of the group try to pick out the false one.

Teaching material

Introduction

- Today we are going to be looking at 'Why and How Should I Read the Bible?'
- Some of you may be proud of the fact that you've never read the Bible. Others may think you know the Bible well. Here is where we find out what you really know.
- I am going to read out a series of quotes, as a group you must decide if you think they are in the Bible or not. (Photocopy sheet 5)
- Lots of people think they know what the Bible says, but unless you read it yourself you will never know for sure.

At this stage it is probably worth giving some very basic information on the Bible for the benefit of those in the group who really have no idea at all what it is all about.

See photocopy sheet 6 and the Youth Alpha guest manuals for ideas.

As we go on with this session we want to look at some reasons why the Bible is the most popular, the most powerful and the most precious book in the world.

1. An instruction manual for life

- Because the Bible is God's book, and because he is our Creator and our loving heavenly Father, it can help to show us how to live our lives in the best possible way (2 Timothy 3:15–17).

- You could say, 'But it is so old! It can't possibly help me with my life in the 21st Century!'

- Let us try to understand how it can help us by looking at the difference between the way a map helps a traveller, and the way a compass helps a traveller.

You will need to bring to the session a local map and a compass.

Spread the map out on the wall.

Ask a volunteer to come up and use the map to find their way from the point 'A' to point 'B' (perhaps their home to the meeting place).

Then ask them how to get from a point 'A' to a point 'B' that are not covered by the map (perhaps their home to the Eiffel Tower or the Statue of Liberty). It is impossible.

- Maps are wonderfully useful inventions and we would be 'lost' without them.

- But, maps are only useful in exactly the right place at exactly the right time.

- If the Bible were like a map it would not be of much use to us today. It would only focus on the culture and customs of the Near East of 2000 years ago. It wouldn't be useful in today's world.

Now, bring out a compass and ask a volunteer to find North with it.

- Compasses don't give as much information as maps.

- However, the good thing about compasses is that they work anywhere (except possibly the North Pole) at any time.

- God has designed the Bible to be much more like a compass than a map. This is why it is still useful to us today in showing us how best to live our lives.

    It provides us with principles that don't change

with time and that help us to make all kinds of decisions. (Give some illustrations that are relevant to your group.)

2. A way to relationship

- But there is even more to the Bible than a source of help in how to live our lives. It's about something even more important than that.

- The Bible is about relationship with God.

- It is like a love letter, text message, fax and e-mail all rolled into one.

- It is the most common and most important way God speaks to us and it is how we get to know him.

- Through the Bible we hear from God and we get to know Jesus.

3. How do we hear God speak through the Bible?

- Choose a time when you are not rushed or stressed – if possible make this a regular habit.

- Choose a place where you are relaxed and where you won't be disturbed (Mark 1:35).

- Begin by praying: ask God to speak to you through what you read.

- Don't just switch off and let your mind wander! Ask yourself: What does this say? What does this mean? How should this affect me?

- Put what you have read and learned into practice.

- Read it, learn from it, but most of all enjoy it!

Activity in small groups

Lego competition

From a local toy or hobby shop buy enough of the smallest Lego kits to give one out to each small group. Hand out the Lego sets you have bought, one to each group. Explain that this is a competition. On the word go the group must build whatever it is in their box as fast as possible. (The trick is that you will have removed the instructions from half of the boxes.) See how the groups get on – the assumption is that the groups that have the instructions will finish the task much more quickly and easily.

Use this as a link to start discussing how the young people feel about following God's instructions for their lives in the Bible.

- Do instructions make you feel controlled or do you find them helpful?
- Do you like the idea of the Bible giving us help about how to make the best of our lives?
- Why do you think God bothered to give us the Bible?

Note: you might like to introduce some contemporary translations of the Bible, and some youth-oriented Bible reading notes at this time.

Photocopy Sheet 6 – Is it in the Bible?

01 In the beginning God created the heavens and the earth

IN (Genesis 1:1)

02 God helps those who help themselves

OUT

03 Cleanliness is next to godliness

OUT

04 You must not steal

IN (Exodus 20:15)

05 There is a time for everything

IN (Ecclesiastes 3:1)

06 Everyone is equal under the sun

OUT

07 Father forgive them for they don't know what they are doing

IN (Luke 23:34)

08 For what we are about to receive, may the Lord make us truly thankful

OUT

09 Money is the root of all evil

OUT
(But, 'the love of money' is described as 'a root of all kinds of evil' 1 Timothy 6:10)

10 Hell hath no fury like a woman scorned

OUT (Shakespeare)

11 Don't judge other people or you will be judged

IN (Matthew 7:1)

12 Turn or burn

OUT

13 Do all you can to lead a peaceful life

IN (1 Thessalonians 4:11)

14 He who would valiant be, 'gainst all disaster

OUT (hymn by John Bunyan)

15 Do not be fooled: you can't cheat God

IN (Galatians 6:7)

Photocopy Sheet 7 – All about the Bible

This big thick book, the Bible, is really a whole library of short books slipped into one cover.

It is divided in two:

★ The Old Testament covers the history of the Israelite people up to the birth of Jesus.

★ The New Testament covers the life of Jesus and his first followers who set up the church.

If we combine both halves there are 66 books in total. Some of these books are like history books; others are full of poetry and love songs.

The Bible can be exciting reading: there is drama, war, love and murder, heroes and heroines, villains and evil kings.

Christians believe that the Bible was written through an amazing partnership between God and its human authors. It really is God's word, but it was also written by real people with their own ideas, words and stories to tell.

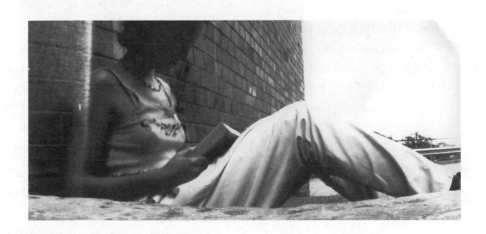

Session 6 – How Does God Guide us?

Arrival game

Bean Blitz

You will need to buy enough jelly-beans to be able to give an envelope or small bag containing 20 beans to every person who arrives and wishes to play.
Once people have their beans the object, naturally, is to obtain more.
You get more beans by approaching another person with a certain number of beans in your closed hand.
You say to the person 'Odd or even?'
The person has the opportunity to guess whether you have an odd or even number of beans in your hand (but they don't have to, if they don't want to).
If they guess correctly they get the beans in your hand.
If they guess incorrectly then you may take from them the number of beans that you have in your hand.
If you run out of beans you are out of the game.
The person with the most beans at the end is the winner.

Introduction to the session

- Welcome the group.

- Today we want to look at how God guides us.

- Many people think that being guided by God must be like guessing at the number of beans in somebody's closed hand – a blind leap in the dark – but it isn't. God has given us many ways of determining what is right. We just have to learn to use them.

Getting to know one another – in small groups

Hand out paper and pens to the group.

They must each note down the answers to the following questions:

1. If I were a dog, I would be a . . .

2. If I were a car, I would be a . . .

3. If I were a kind of music, I would be a . . .

4. If I were an animal in the zoo, I would be a . . .

5. If I were a TV or film character, I would be . . .

Make it clear to the group that the idea is not just to put down their favourite dog, car, music, but to think of a dog, car, or style of music that somehow reflects the kind of person they are. Once everyone has filled in his or her answers, collect in the scraps of paper, then ask each person to take one piece of paper out. When they read out the five answers they have before them the rest of the group must try to guess whose piece of paper it is.

Teaching material

Introduction

This introduction takes place in small groups.
Hand out to each group the small Lego kits that you used during the session on the Bible.
Blindfold one member of the small group.
The blindfolded member is the only person allowed to touch the pieces of the Lego set.
The other members must guide him in which pieces to pick up and how to put them together.
It will be difficult but perhaps, given time, one group might finish the task!

- Learning to receive guidance is a vital part of life. We all need guidance in different areas – from directions on how to get to a friend's house, to advice on which subjects we should continue to study at school.

- God promises to guide us when we ask him.

- God has a good plan for each of us (Psalm 32:8; John 10:3–4; Jeremiah 29:11; Romans 12:2).

- God's guidance is not like a set of rules, or like directions yelled out to us. Instead it comes out of the relationship that we have with him.

- God guides us in many different ways.

For the rest of this talk use short personal testimonies from your team (or from members of the group) to take the place of visual aids or other illustrations. Hearing people's experiences is the best way to learn about God's guidance, and also the best way to build the confidence to allow him to guide us.

You probably won't want to have a testimony for every one of the six methods that God uses, but two or three 'real life stories' will bring this talk to life.

1. Through the Bible

- The Bible is full of general guidelines about how we should live our lives – we should always follow these as they can tell us what is right and wrong and as we read speak to our lives (2 Timothy 3:16).

- God also speaks to us through the Bible about specific situations. If we make a habit of studying the Bible regularly then God will often bring a particular verse to light at just the right time to help guide us in a decision (Psalm 119:105, 130–3).

2. Through the Holy Spirit

- The Holy Spirit – helps us to recognise God's voice (John 10:3–4; Acts 16:7).

3. Through common sense

- Common sense – God wants us to use our brains to think about the consequences of our choices (Psalm 32:8–9).

4. Through advice from others

- The wiser you are the more aware you will be that you need help to make the most of life (Proverbs 12:15; 15:22; 20:18).

5. Through circumstances

- Circumstances – our eyes should be open to opportunities and to closed doors.

- But sometimes we need to keep going in spite of difficulty (Acts 16:7; 1 Corinthians 16:9).

Conclusion

- Don't rush decisions – sometimes we have to wait.

- Remember that we all make mistakes – but God forgives (Joel 2:25).

- Let God guide you and watch your life take off.

Activity in small groups

Photocopy sheet 8 – Who is going to guide you?
Have the group place these sources of guidance, often used by teenagers, in order of usefulness with the most useful at the top and the least useful at the bottom.

Discuss

- Is there anything on this list that you think God would never use to guide us? Why / why not?

- Which sources of guidance would you feel most and least comfortable with?

- Are some sources of more use in certain areas? Which ones in which areas?

- Do you like the thought of being guided by God?

Photocopy Sheet 8 – Who is going to guide you?

Friends	**Research from books or internet**
Problem page of a magazine	Teacher
Priest or minister	**TV**
Parents	**Doctor**
Horoscopes	**The Bible**
Prayer	

Weekend away: Talk 1 – Who Is the Holy Spirit?

Note: It is assumed that these talks will take place on a day or weekend away. Therefore, the usual session outlines are not appropriate, as much of what happens will depend on the type of weekend you are running and your schedule. What follows are the talk outlines and one small group activity designed to follow the 'What Does the Holy Spirit Do?' talk. (Over the weekend, there are usually small groups after this talk and before the final session – but the small group time before the final session is intended to be an opportunity to discuss and reflect upon the group's experiences.)

Teaching material

Introduction

Guess who?

Prior to the weekend take photos or video footage of a number of young people from the group. They should be in disguise – hiding their identities. At the start of this session display the photos or video clips and have the group try to guess who is being featured. For a less labour intensive introduction, photocopy the face of a famous person onto OHP transparency and cover it with a piece of scrap paper. With the young people watching tear off parts of the covering paper, strip by strip, until the group can guess who's face is being projected.

- The Holy Spirit has remained masked and misunderstood for too long.
- He is the third person of the Trinity – Father, Son and Holy Spirit.
- It is easier for us to picture a Father, or Jesus the Son, so we want to ask, 'Who is the Holy Spirit?'
- To do this we are going to take a quick tour through the Bible starting at the very beginning . . .

1. He was involved in creation

Play the breath test game.
Call up four or five volunteers and give each one something strong-tasting to suck or eat.
For example: a clove of garlic; a Fisherman's Friend cough sweet; curry sauce; strong mint; banana.
The rest of the group have to parade past the volunteers and try to guess what they have just eaten by smelling their breath.

- The Holy Spirit is known as the breath of God.
- He was involved in the creation of the universe (Genesis 1:2).
- He breathed life into humans (Genesis 2:7).

2. Particular people, particular times, particular tasks

Produce a plug, the electrical flex to be wired into it and a screwdriver. Ask for a volunteer to come up to the front to wire the plug for you.
As the volunteer is struggling to get all the wires correctly fixed in the right places, say:

- Without a power source a plug is pretty useless.
- The Holy Spirit was a source of power in the Old Testament but only the right person, in the right place, at the right time, received the benefit. (Bezalel, an artist – Exodus 31:1–5; Gideon, a leader – Judges 6:14–16,34; Samson, for strength – Judges 15:14–15; Isaiah, a prophet – Isaiah 61:1–3)

3. The Holy Spirit was promised by the Father

Before the session starts fill a backpack with cans of Coke, or other cartons of drink. At this point in the talk find a volunteer who considers themselves good at doing press-ups. Let them demonstrate a few, and then put the heavy rucksack on their back before they try a few more.
Now show the volunteer, and the rest of the group, what is inside the rucksack.

- What was heavy to carry on the outside, would sustain and empower you if it were inside.

Give out the drinks to the group for them to enjoy as you continue speaking.

- In the Old Testament the covenant (or agreement) between God and his people was an external (outside) one. They had to keep lots of rules, sacrifice lots of animals and it was a burden on them (like carrying the drinks).

- But God promised that the time would come when the agreement would be an internal one – in their hearts – and that to help them keep it the Holy Spirit would come to everyone. When it's inside you the drink is a source of energy (Ezekiel 36:26–27; Joel 2:28–29).

4. Jesus and the Holy Spirit

- Around the time Jesus was on the scene the Holy Spirit became very busy.

- A man called John the Baptist announced that someone was coming who would baptise people not just with water, but with the Holy Spirit – that would be Jesus (Luke 3:16).

- At Jesus' baptism the Holy Spirit came down on him (Luke 3:22), and he received power (Luke 4:1).

- Jesus predicted that his disciples would receive the Holy Spirit, but still they had to wait (John 7:37–39).

Conclusion

- Today the Holy Spirit is available to all of us (Acts 2:38–39).

- He can breathe new life into us and give us power to live for God.

Weekend away: Talk 2 – What Does the Holy Spirit Do?

Teaching material

Introduction

Write out on pieces of paper the members of well-known family groups of three or four. (One piece of paper per member.) For example: David, Victoria, Brooklyn and Romeo Beckham; Homer, Marge, Bart, and Lisa Simpson. Bill, Hilary and Chelsea Clinton. Make yours up from family groups your young people will know. There should be one character for every member of your group. Place each piece of paper inside its own balloon and blow the balloons up. At the start of the session release the balloons. Each member of the group must grab hold of a balloon, burst it, find the name of a family member inside it and then find the other members of their family group.

You now have your group divided down into family groups of three or four. Tape or tie the 'families' together at the wrists (be careful not to hurt – masking tape works well) so that they form family rings. Set them some simple (under normal circumstances) tasks.

For example:　Undo and retie the shoelaces of everyone in the family.
Place lipstick on the girls in the family – and the boys if you like!
Eat a bowl of cornflakes – you decide if it is a good idea to put milk in or not.
Make up your own – whatever would amuse your group.

- In this session we are going to look at the work of the Holy Spirit.
- Just as we are physically born into a human family – so the Holy Spirit gives us a new birth into God's family (John 3:5–7).

1. Sons and daughters of God

Bring in a copy of your birth certificate.
Point out a few details – your full name, your parents, your date and place of birth. The young people will probably be fascinated by this insight into your private life.

- When we become Christians we are born again.
- As babies we had a physical birth this time it is a spiritual birth.
- Our spirit is united with the Holy Spirit and a new creature is born – a child of God.
- This brings immense privileges – after all we are children of the King of Kings.

2. Getting to know God better
- The Holy Spirit also helps us to develop our relationship with our Father God (Ephesians 2:18).
- He helps us to pray, and helps us to discover what God has to say to us in the Bible (Romans 8:26; Ephesians 1:17–18).

3. Growing in the family likeness
See photocopy sheet 9 – Spot the family likeness? See if the young people can pick out who is related to whom.

- Very often in human families there is a family likeness.
- This is also true of God's family.
- As we spend time with God the Holy Spirit changes us to make us more like God.
- The characteristics of God's family are not physical – like big hands or blonde hair.
- The characteristics of God's family are love, joy and peace – the 'fruit of the Spirit' (Galatians 5:22; 2 Corinthians 3:17–18).

4. One big family
- The same Holy Spirit lives inside of every Christian regardless of nationality, church, age, or location.
- We are all one family (Ephesians 4:3–6).

5. Gifts for all the children

- Just like a human parent, God loves to give gifts to his children.

- God also knows that each of his children is different and so he gives different gifts to each child.

- The gifts that God gives us are for us to use to help the rest of the family (1 Corinthians 12:1–11).

6. A growing family

Take a balloon left over from the introduction and blow it up.

- Remember from the last session that the Holy Spirit is known as the breath of God.

- Just as I used my breath to make that balloon grow, so the Holy Spirit is responsible for making God's family grow.

- The Holy Spirit gives us the power to live for Jesus.

- The Holy Spirit gives us the courage to tell others so that they can join the family (Acts 1:8).

Conclusion

- Every Christians has the Holy Spirit living in them.

- Not every Christian is filled with the Holy Spirit.

- The Bible says, 'Be filled with the Spirit'. That is what we are going to talk about in the next session (Ephesians 5:18–20).

Activity in small groups

Give out pens and paper.

- We are going to continue in the theme of family likeness.

On your sheets draw (or if you refuse to draw, write) the characteristics that your family share – the things that make up your family likeness. These do not have to be physical things, like hair colour or face shape, they could also be to do with personality – such as being quick to get angry or quick to laugh; or to do with tastes – we all like watching sport or we all like eating kebabs.

When the young people have had time to do their drawings take a few minutes to discuss what they have put down. Take care to be sensitive. There should not be teasing and if people have written negatively about their families this should be dealt with sensitively. As a group choose one young person to be the group artist.

- Now we are going to return to thinking about the Christian family likeness.
What is it that is characteristic of Christians?

Allow the young people free rein. These do not have to be positive attributes. The group artist should draw symbols or scenes to illustrate what the other members of the group are suggesting.
Finish by talking about which of these things the group think are good and which are not so good. Which things should they be trying to imitate, and which things should they be trying to change about the way the church is perceived?

Note: in the adult Alpha course this is often the point where the gift of tongues is discussed at some length. This is for clarity, and to reassure the members of the group about what might take place in the next session. You might like to bear this in mind for your group.

Photocopy Sheet 9 – Spot the family likeness

Answer: A and B; C and E; D and H; F and G

Weekend away: Talk 3 – How Can I Be Filled with the Holy Spirit?

Introduction

Vacuum experiment

You will need two large soft drink bottles (at least two litre), one should be full, unopened, and the other completely empty but with the top screwed on tight; also, one bowl full of hot water and one bowl full of cold water. Note: the bowls must be big enough to completely submerge the bottle in and the water should be as cold as possible.

Submerge the full bottle in the bowl of hot water for a couple of minutes. Take it out and then plunge it immediately into the bowl of cold water. Hold it there for a couple of minutes. Nothing will happen.

Repeat the process with the empty bottle and after a couple of minutes in cold water it should collapse – crumple in on itself.

See if the scientists in your group can give an explanation.

- The bottle that was filled was stronger.
- To be strong Christians we need to be filled with the Holy Spirit.
- We are going to talk now about how we can be filled with the Holy Spirit.

1. What happens when people experience the Holy Spirit?

- The Book of Acts in the New Testament is the story of the start of the Christian church.
- All through the book there are stories of people being filled with the Holy Spirit.
- Some people were filled as soon as they became Christians and others were filled later on.

Pentecost – Acts 2:2–4
Samaria – Acts 8:14–17
Paul – Acts 9:17–19
Ephesus – Acts 19:1–6

Bring in a gas camping lantern and turn off the lights, darken the room as much as you can.
Start with the gas lantern turned down low:

- As we have said before, all Christians have the Holy Spirit in them.
- The question is, 'How much will we allow the Holy Spirit to fill us?'

Open the valve on the lantern allowing more and more gas to flow until the room becomes brighter and brighter.

- God doesn't want us just to have a little bit of his Spirit; he wants us to be filled so that we burn brightly giving off heat and light to those around us.
- From the book of Acts we can see that things happen when people are filled.
- Here is what happened to Cornelius and his household when they were filled.

  – Power – just as when we turned up the gas, we can normally see something happening when people are filled with Holy Spirit (Acts 10:44–45).

  – Praise – they found new exciting natural ways of praising God (Acts 10:46).

  – New language, sometimes called tongues, another way of praying to God in a language that we don't normally understand but that helps us to communicate directly to God – our spirit direct to his (Acts 10:46).

  – If we want this gift we only have to ask and then do our part by speaking out the new words in the normal way (1 Corinthians 14).

(If you did not do so during the activity/discussion that followed the last session, then this would be a good time to explain more about the gift of tongues.)

2. Can anything stop us being filled?

Buy a heart shaped sponge and have a bowl of water handy.

- God wants to fill all his children with his Holy Spirit, but sometimes we put up barriers that make it difficult for us to be filled. We can be like this sponge that has the capacity to be filled but is hard and resistant.

- We doubt that God wants to give us such a good gift – but he does (Luke 11:9–10).

- We get scared – but God loves us, his gifts are good (Luke 11:11–13).

- We doubt that we're worth giving such a gift to – but God promises to any who ask him (Luke 11:13).

- When we believe that God wants us to have such a good gift it is like water coming and softening this sponge.

Sprinkle water on the sponge until it has become soft.

- Then we are ready to be filled with the Holy Spirit.

Place the sponge in the bowl of water until it is filled with water that pours out of it when you lift it up.

Conclusion

- It is not good enough to talk about being filled with God's Holy Spirit.

- We also need to give God the chance to fill us.

For guidance on leading this time of ministry, please refer to 'Ministry on Youth Alpha' in the Practical Skills section (pp.50–1).

Session 7 – How Can I Resist Evil?

Arrival game

Sticky nose relay

This is a simple team relay where you have to crawl on your hands and knees to retrieve a cotton wool ball from a basket at the other end of the room.

The only thing that makes this relay different from the norm is that you pick up the cotton wool ball using your nose which has been previously coated with Vaseline to make it sticky.

Arrange the players into two or more teams behind the starting line. Place the basket with the cotton wool balls in it at the other end of the room.

Once noses are coated say 'Go!' to start the relay. Contestants must crawl down the room, plunge their noses into the basket until a cotton wool ball attaches itself.

Then with the cotton wool balls on their noses they must crawl back down the course to their team.

When they arrive back they are NOT allowed to use their hands to remove the cotton wool ball from their noses. They can only do so by shaking their heads vigorously. Only when the cotton wool ball is dislodged can the next team member start.

The team with the most cotton wool balls at the end of the time period wins.

Introduction to the session

- Welcome the group

- So far on Youth Alpha we have focused on all the good news – God's love for us, his desire for relationship with us, his willingness to guide us.

- Yet if we are honest, when we look around the world, perhaps even at trouble and difficulty in our own lives, we realise that there is evil in the world as well as good.

- Today we are going to be looking at, 'How can I resist evil?'

Getting to know one another – in small groups

Fire drill

Have the group imagine that their home is on fire. Make clear that all the good advice says that in that situation you should just run for your life, but ask them to imagine that in this special situation they have a few minutes of safety to grab just a few precious items from the flames. Assuming that all people and all animals were already safe, what would you take?

Ask the group to make a list of a few items that they would snatch from the flames. When they have made their lists have them read them out to the rest of the group and then ask some of these questions to get a discussion going.

- What is the most expensive thing that has been saved by the group?

- Has anyone saved anything that belongs to someone else?

- If you had to let one item on your list burn, which item would it be?

- If you could only save one of the items on your list which one would you save?

- Is there anything on your list that has only sentimental value?

Teaching material

Introduction

Caricatures

Do you have access to computer photo software? Or do you have a gifted artist in your group or church? If so, make up some caricatures – either of famous people that will be known by the group, or of actual members of the group. (If you do choose to have someone draw simple caricatures of group members, or if you use computer software to distort photos of group members, make sure that the results are not going to offend or hurt the group members – for example, by playing on a feature the group member might be embarrassed about.)

Spend some time looking at and enjoying the caricatures.

After the game display the typical image of the Devil found on photocopy sheet 10.

- This is also a kind of a caricature: the Devil doesn't really look like this but that doesn't mean that he is not real.

- Christians believe that just as God is the source of all that is good and beautiful so the Devil is behind all evil and horror.

1. Why should we believe in the Devil?

- Because the Bible speaks of him

  – in the Old Testament (Job 1; 1 Chronicles 21:1; Isaiah 14)

  – in the New Testament (Ephesians 6:11–12; 1 Peter 5:8–11)

- Because Christians have believed in him down the ages.

- Because it is clear from the horror and evil in the world that he is at work.

- But it is just as dangerous to take too much of an interest in the Devil as to doubt that he even exists.

2. What does the Devil have to do with me?

- The Devil aims to destroy all humans (John 10:10).

- He tries to blind our eyes so that we cannot see God.

- He tries to feed doubts into our minds.

- He tries to tempt us to do wrong. (See Genesis 3, for examples of all of the above.)

3. Should I be worried?

The point that we want to communicate is that as Christians we have been transferred from the Devil's kingdom of darkness to Jesus' kingdom of light and life. Therefore, we are now under Jesus' authority not the Devil's. We will be using a skit/role-play, based upon the football world's practice of player transfers from one club to another to illustrate this (photocopy sheet 11). If you wish you can rehearse this in advance with a few members of the group, but if you pick confident volunteers it should also be possible to do it ad-lib in front of the group. Knowing your young people, make a decision about what will be most likely to work out well and amusingly.

After the skit:

- Explain that as Christians we are transferred from the Devil's team to Jesus' team. Now Jesus is in charge of us, not the Devil (Colossians 1:13).

- Jesus has completely defeated Satan and won the war but there are still battles going on and as soldiers in God's army we are involved in these (Colossians 2:15; Luke 10:17–20).

4. How do we defend ourselves?

- The book of Ephesians in the New Testament describes the armour that God has given us:

  – the belt of truth – knowing Jesus' truth to counter the Devil's lies (Ephesians 6:14)

  – the breastplate of righteousness – believing Jesus can protect us from guilt (Ephesians 6:14)

  – the boots of the gospel of peace – being ready to speak about Jesus (Ephesians 6:15)

  – the shield of faith – being sure of God's promises (Ephesians 6:16)

  – the helmet of salvation – protecting our minds from doubts (Ephesians 6:17)

  – the sword of the Spirit – getting to know the Bible and attacking the Devil with its truth (Ephesians 6:17)

5. How do we attack?

- By praying – the Devil trembles when we pray (2 Corinthians 10:4).

- By action – we attack the Devil by doing the things that Jesus told us to do (Luke 7:22).

Conclusion

- The Devil is real and so is his influence in the world, but he is no match for God. There is no comparison between them. It is a worse mismatch than your pet goldfish fighting against a great white shark.

- We have no cause to fear the Devil because we are now in Jesus' kingdom.

- There is no reason for great interest in the Devil. Why worry about a loser?

Activity – in small groups

Hand out newspapers to the group. Have them cut out photos from the negative stories that they find. Stick these photos onto a sheet of paper. Choose a few of the photos that appear interesting and ask these questions: Who is it that is suffering in this story?

Who is to blame?

A   The people who are suffering

B   People that are causing the suffering

C   God

D   Devil

E   Other

What is the cause of this situation?

A   The evil (sin) done by humanity in general

B   The evil (sin) done by those involved in this particular situation

C   Evil generally

Is it right to blame the Devil for everything that goes wrong in the world?

Is it right to blame the Devil for everything that goes wrong in our lives?

Photocopy Sheet 10 – Devil caricature

Photocopy Sheet 11 – Transfer Skit

Script

Scene 1 – The newsroom

Sports anchorman – Good evening and welcome to Channel 5's sports report. The big news tonight is of a rumoured transfer. Rotundo, Brazil's leading striker and scorer of the winning goal in the last world cup, could be leaving Inferno FC to play for the Saints. While we're here why don't we look at that goal one more time and remind ourselves what all of the fuss is about. *(Points to his left)*

Commentator – And Rotundo is off, barrelling down the wing. . . . beats one with some silky skills, plays it past the second defender and sprints onto the ball. Now he's in lots of space. Fakes the long cross and instead takes it into the box himself – oh this is too much, fantastic skills, amazing footwork, such confidence! And now it's only the goalkeeper to beat. Rotundo draws back his powerful right foot, shoots . . . scorcher . . . the goalkeeper's not even moved . . . goal!
(At the same time as the commentator is commentating Rotundo is acting out everything the commentator is saying.)

Sports anchorman – Well, I think that says it all and I never tire of watching that clip. I think that we can safely say there are going to be some very excited Saints fans tonight as they contemplate the difference Rotundo could make to their club's chances of winning the championship.

Scene 2 – A press conference

Reporter – Rotundo how does it feel to be one of the Saints now?

Rotundo – Amazing, I can't tell you how glad I am to be free of Inferno. It feels like a new life to me. I can't tell you how bad our old manager, Lucius, treated us. Anyone would have thought he hated us. He always made us play with injuries, trained us too hard, punished us when we lost and dropped us when we won. It was hell.

Second reporter – How does it feel to be the most expensive transfer ever?

Rotundo – I'm just thrilled that the manager here at the Saints felt I was worth it.

Scene 3 – Rotundo's mansion in the middle of the night

(A phone rings beside the bed. Rotundo picks it up.)

Rotundo – Huh?! Who's calling?

Lucius – Rotundo? Rotundo? This is your manager speaking, you useless lump of lard. Why haven't you been training?

Rotundo – Lucius? Is that you? It's the middle of the night . . .

Lucius – . . . not here in Brazil, it's not. I don't know what you're doing on the other side of the world anyway. Get back here!

Rotundo – But I'm not your player anymore! You can't order me around. The Saints bought me and now I play for them. Now get off the phone!

The end

Session 8 – Why and How Should I Tell Others?

Arrival game

Water balloon throw

Split everyone who would like to play into pairs. All the 'ones' stand shoulder to shoulder facing in one direction. All the 'twos' stand opposite their partners, facing them toe-to-toe.

Give a water balloon to each of the ones.

At the command 'Go!' the 'ones' must pass the balloon to the 'twos'. Assuming they all accomplish this successfully both the ones and the twos take a step backwards. On 'Go!' the 'twos' must now toss the balloon back to the 'ones'. If anybody drops the balloon, or if the balloon bursts as it is caught that pair is eliminated.

Every time a pair successfully completes a throw and a catch they must both take a step backwards. The winning pair is the pair that lasts the longest or manages a successful throw and catch at the greatest distance.

Introduction to the session

- Welcome the group.
- We are going to be talking about how we discuss our faith with other people, 'How and why should we tell others?'

Getting to know one another – in small groups

Today each small group will be developing and practising a short skit/role-play to be used as an illustration in the coming teaching section of the session.

There are five role-plays – if you have five groups you are laughing. If you have less you will need to assign more than one role-play to each group. If you have more you will be able to enjoy the different interpretations of the same scenarios. The five role-plays are given on photocopy sheet 12.

Teaching material

Introduction

Best to worst

Give each of the young people a copy of photocopy sheet 13, or copy it onto acetate and use an OHP. You should use it to lead an open discussion on which are the best and the worst ways of talking about our faith.

- We can do it well or we can do it badly, but the fact is that Christians are told by Jesus to tell others – everyone needs to know that nothing in life can make them truly happy without a friendship with God (Matthew 28:16–20).
- How can we do the best possible job of telling people about Jesus?
- The people that we have a responsibility to tell about Jesus are those that we have relationship with.
- Fortunately, there are plenty of ways of telling others about your faith.

1. Live the message

Role-play 1 – Actions speak louder than words

- The way that we live is more important than the words we speak (Matthew 5:13–16).

2. Talk the message

Role-play 2 – You don't need all the answers

- Not everybody who asks us a question about Christianity is really interested in the answer. They might just be trying to show off or looking for an argument.
- If we can see that it actually matters to the person asking we should try to answer, either right then or later when we've had a chance to talk to another Christian about it or look it up in a book

(2 Corinthians 5:11).

- Don't worry if you don't know the answer but do be willing to go away and find out.

3. Present the message

Role-play 3 – What are you doing on Friday night?

- Sometimes we will have the opportunity to explain all about Christianity to an interested friend or relative.

- Sometimes it is easier and better to invite them to a special event where someone else can present the good news in a clear and exciting way (John 1:39–42).

4. Power the message

Role-play 4 – What I have I give you

- That role-play was straight from the book of Acts in the Bible. God often used miracles to back up the message – it makes it much easier to convince people (Acts 3).

- God still does miracles today and we shouldn't be afraid to ask him to show his power and make himself known to people.

5. Pray the message

Role-play 5 – It doesn't work without a power source

- Prayer is like the power source to any attempt to tell people the good news about Jesus.

- If we haven't been praying then things won't work.

- Pray that people's eyes would be opened to see the truth about God (2 Corinthians 4:4).

- Pray that God would give us boldness to talk about our faith (Acts 4:29–31).

Conclusion

- Which would you rather have: £10,000 every day for twenty days or £1 that doubles its cumulative value every day for twenty days?

If they are smart they will choose the £1 which will earn them £524,288 not just £200,000.

- It is easy to think I could never be a great preacher so there's no point my making any

effort to talk about Jesus to my friends. What difference could I make?

- That's wrong: just as the £1 that kept doubling grew bigger than the £10,000 every day, so too if we all just brought one friend to Jesus each year, and helped them to bring one of their friends the next year we would see huge numbers of young people coming to Jesus.

- Could you commit to doing one of these in the next week?

  – Ask a friend to a youth event.

  – Pray for a friend.

  – Make an effort to talk to a lonely person at school.

  – Tell somebody the story of how you came to be a Christian.

- Never give up (Romans 1:16).

- We might never know the effect of something that we have said or done, but God will use our lives and our words if we trust him.

Activity in small groups

The activity today will be at the very end of the session and with everyone together.

First, take a little time with the small group to think about what has been discussed.

You might want to talk about friends who are not Christians and about what would be good ways of bringing the good news to them.

Closing – Light of the world

In as quiet and reflective an atmosphere as is possible with your group give out a candle to each person and darken the room. Light a candle and use it to light the candles of the people immediately on either side of you. They in turn light their neighbours candle and so on until the whole group has their candles alight.

This is probably most powerful without explanation. The young people will be able to make the connections for themselves, but you might like to finish with a prayer.

Note: younger youth love fire. You need to be very watchful if you use this closing activity. Be aware of the temptations the candles might present to some of your young people!

Photocopy Sheet 12 – Telling others role plays

Here is a list of five role-plays or skits. Your small group will be assigned at least one of them to practice before acting it out to the rest of the group later. The titles and ideas given here are only suggestions. Look at the theme of the skit and then find the best way possible to act that out. Make it as relevant to real life as possible.

Role-play 1 – Actions speak louder than words

Theme – when we are telling others what we do / how we act is often far more important than what we say. Ideas – show someone being positively affected by an act of kindness, or by someone's behaviour.

Role-play 2 – You don't need all the answers

Theme – telling others is not about being a brilliant theologian who knows everything about everything. It is about helping others to find answers to questions that really bother them or keep them from believing. Ideas – show a discussion and try to illustrate how some questions are just about trying to show off and look clever, while others are really important.

Role-play 3 – What are you doing on Friday night?

Theme – often it is easier to take a friend to hear a presentation of Christianity than it is to explain everything ourselves. Ideas – show a Christian trying to pluck up courage to invite his friend to a Christian youth event.

Role-play 4 – What I have I give you

Theme – this role-play is taken directly from the New Testament. It shows how miracles and demonstrations of God's power can help in telling others. Ideas – read Acts 3:1–10 and make up a sketch based on this. It could be set in modern times.

Role-play 5 – It doesn't work without a power source

Theme – prayer is the power source for telling others. If there is no prayer then there is no power in our attempts to tell others. Ideas – you could make up a skit about something running out of power (a computer or a car, for example) and about reconnecting it to the power source to make it work again.

Photocopy Sheet 13 – Best and worst

Active Stream

Session 9 – Does God Heal Today?

Arrival game

Tail grab

Form the young people that want to play into groups of six to ten.

Each group forms a 'snake' as each person puts their arms around the waist of the person in front. The person at the back of the snake then has a handkerchief, or a strip of cloth tucked into his or her belt. This is the tail.

The object of the game is to grab the tail off of the other snakes without losing yours. Only the head of the snake can do the snatching and the snake must remain whole at all times.

Give the command 'Go!' and watch the mayhem!

Introduction to the session

- Welcome the group.
- Ask if anyone is injured after the rough and tumble of the tail grab game.
- Of course you hope not, but in any case today you are going to be talking about healing.

Getting to know one another – in small groups

As we move into the last sessions of the course the games and activities focus on the young people commenting on one another. It is important that the group leader encourages and maintains a positive atmosphere.

Give photocopy sheet 14 out to each young person along with a pen. Ask them to read through the list and jot down beside the different hats the name of somebody in the small group whose personality would be suited by that hat. (Their comments should be positive and upbuilding.)

When they are finished each young person takes it in turns to sit in silence while the rest of the group explain which hats they picked for this young person and why.

Teaching material

Introduction

Play a question and answer game on first-aid and illnesses.

Invite an individual or small group of young people to the front. Explain that you are going to give them a scenario of a medical emergency. They must explain how they would act in that situation. According to how closely their plans mirror those in the 'correct procedure', you will award them between one and five points. The individual or team that is awarded the most points wins.

Scenario 1 – Nosebleed

Correct procedure:
- Tilt head forward.
- Pinch the fleshy part of the nose.
- Give tissues and bowl to contain blood.
- If nosebleed continues beyond 30 minutes take person to hospital.

Scenario 2 – Serious Cut

Correct procedure:
- Place dressing or clean cloth over wound.
- Apply pressure.
- Elevate the affected part of body if possible.
- Take the person to hospital.

Scenario 3 – Choking

Correct procedure:
- Bend person over .
- Apply five sharp slaps on the back between the shoulder blades.
- If the obstruction remains call an ambulance.

- The medical knowledge we have today is a gift from God.

- However, there is another way to approach an illness or injury. Alongside doing all that is medically correct we can pray to God and ask that he would heal miraculously.

- Does God still heal today? Why should we expect him to?

1. Healing in the Bible

- Old Testament: God promises to heal (Exodus 23:25–26; Psalm 41:3).
  God said it was part of his character to heal (Exodus 15:26).
  There are examples of God healing (2 Kings 5; Isaiah 38–39).

- New Testament: The example of Jesus – 25 per cent of the Gospels are about healing.
  The teaching of Jesus – healing as sign of the kingdom (Mark 1:14).

The kingdom of God – key illustration

- This is a term that Jesus used (Mark 1:14).

- It was the basis of his healing ministry.

- It explains a lot about the experience of healing that we have today.

See photocopy sheet 15 – illustration of the now and the not yet aspect of the kingdom of God.

2. Healing in history

Read this story, with as much drama and horror as possible.

- There have been examples of healing and miracles all through the history of the Christian church.

- Augustine of Hippo (the place not the animal), one of the greatest theologians of the first four centuries of the church, showed that he wasn't squeamish by writing this story down for our edification.

A man St Augustine was staying with, called Innocentius, was being treated by doctors for 'fistulae' of which he had 'a large number intricately seated in his rectum'! He had undergone one very painful operation. It was not thought that he would survive another. While St Augustine and others prayed for him, Innocentius was thrown to the floor as if someone had hurled him violently to earth. He groaned and sobbed and his whole body shook so much that he couldn't talk.

The dreaded day of the operation came. 'The surgeons arrived . . . the frightful instruments are produced . . . the part is bared; the surgeon . . . with knife in hand, eagerly looks for the sinus that is to be cut. He searches for it with his eyes; he feels for it with his finger' . . . He found a perfectly healed wound. God had healed Innocentius, much to Innocentius' relief! (Nicky Gumbel, *Alpha - Questions of Life*, Kingsway, p.218)

3. How do we pray for healing?

- God still heals today. Testimony. (Someone you can call upon or a well documented story.)

If you plan to have a time of praying for healing then quickly run through these points. For guidance on how to lead this you could also consult the ministry part of the practical skills section.

- Jesus healed people because he loved them (Mark 1:41; Matthew 9:36).

- It is important that we care and want the best for anyone we pray for.

- Prayers for healing should be simple, not long and complicated.

- The Holy Spirit might guide us in how to pray
  – with a picture in our minds
  – with a sympathy pain
  – with a strong feeling
  – with words in our minds
  – with words for us to speak

- When we pray we should:
  – Ask where it hurts, how long it has hurt, and why it hurts.
  – Pray that God would heal in the name of Jesus.

- Ask that the Holy Spirit would heal the person.

- Continue to be open to more guidance from the Holy Spirit.

- Afterwards we should:

  - Ask the person how they feel.

  - Make sure that they are happy and understand all that has happened.

- Doctors don't have a 100 per cent success rate but they don't stop being doctors and they don't stop trying.

- If we never pray for anyone then nobody will ever be healed.

Activity in small groups

Finish the session with a workshop where you pray for one another.

Only you know if your group is ready for this, but remember: faith is spelt R I S K.

Conclusion

- Earlier we talked about the kingdom of God and we saw that we are living in the between times, where God's kingdom is here but not in all its power and glory.

- God does heal, but not every person and not every time.

Photocopy Sheet 14 – Hats

Pith helmet / safari hat   – for the adventure lover

Veil   – for the intriguing, silent type

Mexican sombrero   – for the happy go lucky, easy going drifter

Baseball cap   – for the sporty type

Cowboy hat   – for the tough, open country type

Hard hat   – for the don't-mind-getting-my-hands-dirty, hard worker

Police helmet   – tough, tackles the difficult problems

Fireman's helmet   – for the thrill seeker

Crash helmet   – for someone that lives his or her life at a frightening pace

Nurse's hat   – for someone who is caring and compassionate

Paper Party hat   – for the good time, party animal

Mortar board   – for the thinker, the student, the intellectual

Bowler hat   – for the sharp business mind

Bandana   – for the cool type that loves to be part of the gang

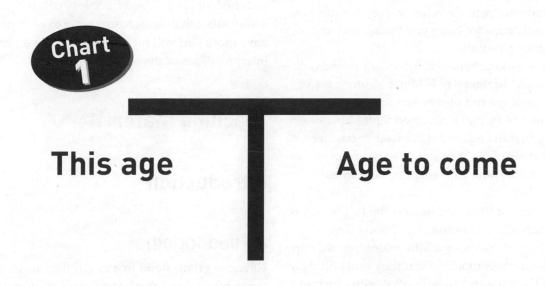

Chart 1

This age | Age to come

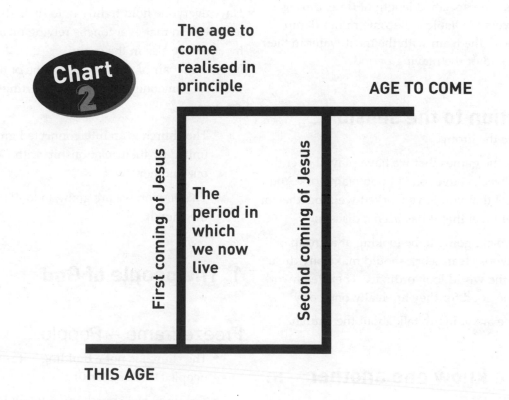

Chart 2

The age to come realised in principle

AGE TO COME

First coming of Jesus

The period in which we now live

Second coming of Jesus

THIS AGE

Session 10 – What about the Church?

Arrival game

Assuming that you 'run' the relay with two teams you will need plastic cups for everyone taking part and four buckets or other receptacles.

Each team has two buckets, one full of water and one empty. The object of the relay is to get as much water as possible out of the full bucket and into the empty one. The difficulty factor is increased tenfold because the only way that the teams are allowed to transfer water is in a chain, from person to person, from cup to cup, and at all times the cups must be held in the players' mouths.

The first member of the team, nearest the full bucket is the only person allowed to use their hands. They can pick up the bucket and pour a little water into the cup held dangling in their mouth. Then they must tilt their head so that the water is poured out of their cup into the waiting cup of the person next to them, who will need to crouch slightly to make sure that their cup is lower. This proceeds on down the line until the last team member tips what remains of the water into the empty bucket.

This continues for a specified length of time, during which the players are liable to become rather damp, and the winner is the team with the most water in their buckets at the end of the playing period.

Introduction to the session

- Welcome the group.
- Many of the games that we have played over the last few weeks have relied upon teamwork. You might feel that you have worked well together, or you might feel that it has been a disaster.
- Today we are going to be looking at a group of people whose teamwork should make any dream team in the world look ordinary. Their teamwork should be good for they are really one body.
- Today we are going to talk about the church.

Getting to know one another – in small groups

In your small groups prepare one of the freeze frames given on photocopy sheet 16.

There are five freeze frames – if you have five groups you are laughing. If you have less you will need to assign more than one freeze frame to each group. If you have more you will be able to enjoy the different interpretations of the same freeze frames.

Teaching material

Introduction

All tied together

Have the group stand in a circle. If there are more than ten to fifteen have them form more than one circle. Pass a ball of thick string or twine from person to person back and forth, across and around the circle. Every young person should be holding onto a piece of string that comes from someone else in the group and goes on to another person. This should create a web like effect. Have everyone hold tightly onto their string and then lean back so that everyone is relying on and supported by everyone else in the group.

Now use a pair of scissors to cut one of the strands of the web. Someone will fall away starting a chain reaction.

- The church is an interconnected group of people, united by their relationship with God and with one another.
- This session we are going to look more closely at the church.

1. The people of God

Freeze frame – People

- The church is not a building – it is made up of people (1 Peter 2:9–10).
- The universal church includes all believers that have ever lived anywhere in the world at any time.

- Today the church is huge – 1,900,000,000 people, more than 34 per cent of the world's population.

2. The family of God

Freeze frame – The perfect family

- When we become Christians we become children of God (Ephesians 2:14–18).
- God is our Father.
- Jesus prayed that we would all be unified.
- We are brothers and sisters and we relate to God and to one another in the church.

3. The body of Christ

Freeze frame – The human machine

- We are all one in the Holy Spirit, just as different parts make up one body (1 Corinthians 12:1–26).
- We all have different gifts from God, just as different parts of the body have different roles.
- We all need each other, just as the different body parts need each other.

4. A holy temple

Freeze frame – The temple

- There is only one church building in the New Testament and that is a special kind of building made of people, not of bricks or other materials (Ephesians 2:19–22).
- All together we make up a holy temple that God loves more than any beautiful cathedral.

5. The bride of Christ

Freeze frame – The bride

- In the New Testament the church is also described as the Bride of Christ (Ephesians 5:25–27, 32).

- Jesus loves his church like a groom loves his bride.
- We, the church, should respond to Jesus by living holy lives, worshipping him, and telling others about him.

Conclusion

- The church is about people: people in relationship with Jesus; people working together; people looking after one another; people serving and sharing good news with others.

To illustrate the importance of being involved with a local church you might like to use the old but effective illustration of the coal taken from the fire at this concluding point. If by some miracle you've not heard it, the story relates that a red-hot coal taken out of the fire and placed on the hearth will soon go cold, even while all the other coals still in the fire are burning brightly.

Activity – in small groups

For this activity to work each small group will need to be in its own room. Should this not be possible you might want to have one group perform the simulation while the others watch and then return to the small groups to discuss it. The simulation requires eight people. If you wish to play with more you may play in pairs or groups sharing the same role. If there are less than eight, the roles of B and G; C and H; D and E may be combined with only slight adaptation (see below).

Church simulation

Instructions for the leaders:

- Hide a can of mandarin oranges somewhere near the window.
- Hide a can opener near the door.
- Hide a spoon near the light switch.

The items should be out of sight but not difficult to find. If other locations are more convenient then adapt the instructions that follow to fit.

- Cut out the eight role descriptions, as set out on photocopy sheet 17.
  Remember you will have to change these if you have used different locations.
- Explain that the object of the game is to give the

leader a spoonful of their favourite snack. They will need help as their hands are tied behind their back.

- Each player needs a file card with their instructions, which they should read and then put away without showing anyone else.

- Encourage the group not to bend the rules by gesturing or muttering.

Set the game in motion and do not interrupt it again unless the participants are struggling so badly that they are giving up hope. The key player is the speaker. It is absolutely essential that role be given to someone who is an imaginative thinker, and good leader. He or she needs to identify what everyone else can and cannot do and give directions.

After the simulation, discuss the frustration of being dependent on others as well as the elation of achievement. How do the young people think this might relate to the session you have just had about the church?

Photocopy Sheet 16 – Freeze frames

Freeze frames are like drama skits frozen in time, like photos of a key moment. The challenge is to portray all that you want to with no movement and no speech.

Freeze frame 1

People

A crowd scene – try to put as much energy, as much feeling of being crammed together with a mass of others into your freeze frame as you can.
You might want to consider being a crowd at a football match, or at a concert, but it's up to you – make it something great!

Freeze frame 2

The family

How do you portray a family without speaking or moving. That is your challenge. You might want to consider the family sitting down at dinner, or posing for an official portrait. (Who's going to play the dog?)

Freeze frame 3

The human machine

You have a special privilege, you are a freeze frame that is allowed to move (So not a freeze frame at all really!) Your challenge is to construct a human machine with moving parts that drive other parts that drive other parts and so on. We want pistons, wheels, cranks and pumps all working together in perfect unison.

Freeze frame 4

The temple

You must build a building using only your bodies – and it mustn't fall down because if you fall you are moving and it's not a freeze frame.
You could do something boring like a pyramid, but why not be adventurous, let's have people sitting on other people's shoulders, let's have a bit of danger! Somehow arrange yourselves into something that is recognisable as a building – you can do it!

Freeze frame 5

The bride

You must create a freeze frame of a wedding scene. Choose the key moment – the bride coming up the aisle, the bride and groom standing in front of the minister, the bride and groom emerging covered in confetti.

Whatever scene you choose you need to be able to make it obvious to the rest of the group exactly what is happening without the use of either movement or words.

Photocopy Sheet 17 – Church simulation

A. You are the speaker. You may talk as much as you like, but you may not move.

B. The only words you may use are 'Yes', 'No', 'I know' and 'I don't know'. You may not move. The can of mandarins is hidden near the window.

C. The only words you may use are 'Yes', 'No', 'I know' and 'I don't know'. You may not move. The can opener is hidden near the door.

D. The only words you may use are 'Yes', 'No', 'I know' and 'I don't know'. You may not move. The spoon is hidden near the light switch.

E. The only words you may use are 'Yes', 'No', 'I know' and 'I don't know'. You may move, but only when you are absolutely sure where the can of mandarins, the can opener and the spoon are. You are allowed to touch and carry them, but you must not take them near the leader.

F. The only words you may use are 'Yes', 'No', 'I know' and 'I don't know'. You may only move if you have the can of mandarins in your hand. You are not allowed to touch anything else that contains metal.

G. The only words you may use are 'Yes', 'No', 'I know' and 'I don't know'. You may only move if you have the can opener in your hand. You are not allowed to touch anything else that contains metal.

H. The only words you may use are 'Yes', 'No', 'I know' and 'I don't know'. You may only move if you have the spoon in your hand. You are not allowed to touch anything else that contains metal.

Weekend away: Talk 4 – How Can I Make the Most of the Rest of My Life?

Introduction

Rising and falling

Place a number of sultanas into a glass filled with lemonade. They will rise and then fall, rise and then fall.

- Life can be like that can't it? Highs and lows. It's no wonder – we get no mocks, trials or practice runs at life – so how can we be sure of making the most of it?

Read: Romans 12:1–21

1. What should we do?

- The way to make the most of our lives is to give them to God.

- Make a break with the past – don't be squeezed into the mould that makes you like everyone else.

- When we become Christians we have a chance to wipe the page clean of past mistakes and start again.
  To illustrate this visually, write or type words onto a whiteboard, OHP or computer. Eg 'said something mean about my friend'. Then erase them completely.

- Make a new start – let God transform you from the inside out (Romans 12:2).

2. How do we do it?

- We must make a decision to offer every part of our lives to God (Romans 12:1).

Illustration

This point takes the young people through the different areas of their life that they can/should commit to God if they want to make the most of their lives.

Before the start of the session dress-up and prepare a member of the group with the following props:
- a watch or clock

- a tool of a trade or career: briefcase, stethoscope, hammer and nails

- a wallet, perhaps stuffed with pretend money

- a fake pair of ears, or else ear muffs, or ear plugs

- joke glasses with bloodshot eyeballs attached, or sunglasses

- long role of thin red paper to be a fake tongue that lolls out when mouth is opened

- fake rubber hand that comes off when you shake hands with someone

- perhaps a strategically placed fig leaf to illustrate sexuality

- a mask

If you're stuck for inspiration visit your local joke or fancy dress shop.
Set up a table to represent an altar. As the items are removed from the volunteer, pile them up on the table to show that they are being given to God.

We present to God our

- time – take off the watch. How do we use our time? How would God have us use it?

- ambitions – remove the briefcase or whatever. Are our goals God's goals for us?

- money – take out the wallet. How do we use what we have? Selfishly or by giving?

- ears – remove the ears. Do we choose to listen to gossip, or believe the best about others?

- eyes – take off fake eyes. What do we chose to look at and watch – particularly on TV or in magazines?

- mouth/tongue – remove fake tongue. The tongue is very powerful. What do we say?

- hands – remove fake hands. Do we give or do we take with our hands and skills?

- sexuality – remove fig leaf. God has made us sexual and he knows how best it can be a pleasure to us.

- masks – remove mask. We all choose to live behind masks some of the time, feeling that people will like us better if we act like the kind of person we think that they want us to be. In fact this prevents us from making true friendships. God wants us to take off our masks.

Conclusion – Why should we do it?

- Because God has a great plan for our future and this is the way to follow it (Romans 12:2).

- Because of all that God has done for us – we owe it to him (Romans 12:1 – 'in view of God's mercy').

LITE STREAM
SESSION OUTLINES

General information

Arrival – opener

The arrival opener for this stream is simply a visual image with a statement or question implicitly or explicitly posed. The opener could be projected from a computer screen, or an OHP, or could simply be photocopied and handed out to guests as they arrive. It is just an 'attention-grabber' – don't feel that you have to comment on it or make further use of it if you don't want to.

If you would like a more dynamic opener to the session you might like to choose a video clip from the corresponding session in the 'Alpha-Tech' stream, or an activity or illustration from the 'Alpha-Active' stream.

Storytelling – in small groups

This section of the session is intended to give the guests a chance to talk about themselves and their own lives. The goal is that this time of listening to their 'stories' should convey the value that we (and indeed God) place upon them. While this is in no way intended as a trick or trade-off (far from it!) it is generally true that if you feel you are being listened to, you are more willing to listen to others.

The theme of the stories the guests are invited to tell also relates to the content of the session.
It is essential that no one feels coerced or put under pressure to speak. Especially in the first few weeks it will be the group leader's role to kick-start this part of the session, either by telling their own story, or by selecting someone else with the confidence (perhaps even speaking to them in advance) to do so. As the weeks go past other members of the group will feel more free to speak up. Encourage as many members of the group as possible to tell their stories.

It is assumed that in most instances a Youth Alpha course using the Alpha-Lite stream will have only a small number of participants – probably not more than one small group. However, if your group is larger than 10 or 12 it would be a good idea to split down into multiple smaller groups for this part of the session, and for the discussion later. To avoid too much coming and going (unless the group is very large) you could probably all stay together for the 'Responding to the Story' section.

Story presentation

As previously noted, one of the key goals for this stream is that the minimum preparation time and presentation skills be required of the person leading. Rather than expect the leader to prepare a talk and then stand up in front of the group and present it, this stream uses written stories and then a short paragraph presenting some of the Youth Alpha teaching material. Both can be read straight from the page with no preparation required.

Story has been chosen because it is a very non-threatening approach, and an approach that is well suited to the post-modern mindset of those that might be wary of in-your-face, black-and-white teaching. This is by no means a cop-out. It is worth noting that a high percentage of the Bible is narrative. God knows that stories communicate and challenge.

Responding to the story

The questions in this section are aimed at helping the guests interact with the story and relate it to their own lives and beliefs. It should also set up the questions that are to be addressed in the teaching section.

Teaching material

This is the section where Alpha content is introduced to the group. Obviously, this is in a very truncated and simple form. Only the basic point of the Alpha session is presented. This is for two reasons. Most often the time constraints of running a course in a school are greater than in other contexts. It is also likely that those on the course have less previous exposure to Christianity than those taking the course in a church or youth club setting.

Discussion in small groups

This is perhaps the key section of the whole session. This is where the guests have the opportunity to engage with the good news of Jesus Christ. Allow people plenty of opportunity to express their opinions and to talk openly and honestly without fear of being considered 'wrong' or 'difficult'.

Closing

The closings suggested are optional. Whether they are appropriate will very much depend on the atmosphere and character of your group. Do not feel that you are failing if the group does not seem ready for this kind of activity.

Introductory session –
Is There More to Life than This?

(Note: This introductory session has been compiled with school assemblies in mind. It might also be used in a classroom, at a meeting of the Christian Union or at any kind of event put on to advertise the Youth Alpha course.)

Introduction

Quotes, jokes and stories about church. Use these or come up with some of your own.

A vicar was taking a small boy around his church and showing him the memorials.
'These are the names of those who died in the services,' said the vicar.
'Did they die at the morning or at the evening service?' asked the boy.

'If all the people who fell asleep in church on Sunday morning were laid out end to end . . . they would be a great deal more comfortable.' – Abraham Lincoln

'I have been to church today, and am not depressed.' – Stated with shock and disbelief, in the diary of Robert Louis Stevenson.

From church notice boards:
'Don't let worry kill you – let the church help!'

'Tonight's sermon topic will be, "What is hell?" Come early and listen to our choir practise.'

Survey – Part 1

- I am going to ask you to answer three questions related to your feelings about Christianity.
- Number one – put your hands in the air if you think Christianity is boring.
  (Estimate the percentage of the group that have their hands in the air.)
- Number two – put up your hands if you think the claims of Christianity are untrue.

(Estimate the percentage of the group that have their hands in the air.)
- Number three – put up your hands if you think that Christianity is irrelevant to the life of a modern young person.
  (Estimate the percentage of the group that have their hands in the air.)

Note down the percentages. If you like you could note them somewhere visible to the group.

Story

Read this story:
Did you hear about the English lady who wanted to buy a house in a remote village in Switzerland? On her return home she realised that she hadn't seen a toilet in her new house. So she wrote to the Swiss estate agent asking about the location of the WC. The estate agent's knowledge of the English language was limited and so he asked the parish priest to translate the letter for him. The only meaning for WC that the priest could think of was related to 'Chapel' – perhaps the lady meant Wayside Chapel or Wesleyan Chapel? As a result this is the reply received by the English lady from the estate agent.

My Dear Madam
I take great pleasure in informing you that the WC is situated nine miles from the house in a beautiful grove of pine trees surrounded by lovely grounds.

It is capable of holding 229 people and it is open on Sundays and Thursdays only. As there are a great number of people expected during the summer months, it is an unfortunate situation, especially if you are in the habit of going regularly. It may interest you to know that my daughter was married in the WC and it was there that she met her husband. I can remember the rush there was for seats. There were ten people to every seat usually occupied by one.

You will be glad to hear that a good number of people bring their lunch and make a day of it, while those who can afford to go by car arrive just in time. I would especially recommend your ladyship to go on Thursdays when there is an organ accompaniment. The acoustics are excellent, even the most delicate sounds can be heard everywhere.

The newest addition is a bell donated by a wealthy resident of the district. It rings every time a person enters. A bazaar is to be held to provide plush seats for all, since the people feel it is long needed. My wife is rather delicate and she cannot attend regularly. It is almost a year since she went last, and naturally it pains her very much not to be able to go more often.

I shall be delighted to reserve the best seat for you, where you shall be seen by all. For the children, there is a special day and time so that they do not disturb the elders. Hoping to be of some service to you.

Yours faithfully.

- That last story is an illustration of how easy it is to get the wrong idea from limited information and then jump to the wrong conclusion with quite spectacular results.

- Many young people have come to the conclusion that church and Christianity are boring, untrue and irrelevant to their lives.

- But what if they have jumped to the wrong conclusion? It could be embarrassing.

Visual illustration

Photocopy sheet 18 shows pictures of young Christians from all over the world, with the comment 'It's not boring, untrue or irrelevant to me'. It can be photocopied onto acetate and projected on an OHP. Perhaps the organisers of the Alpha in the school, or other students, would also be willing to be identified as young people who don't believe that Christianity is boring, untrue and irrelevant.

Challenge

- There are literally millions of young people from all over the world who do not think of

Christianity as boring, untrue and irrelevant.

Read John 14:6

- On the contrary, they believe Jesus and think that Christianity

  - Is the way to a life full of purpose and meaning – and fun

  - Is the truth that can help us to make sense of the confusing world around us

  - Is the life that helps us to choose good over evil and will make us live forever

- In the light of the fact that millions of young people of your age follow Jesus and call themselves Christians, are you certain that you are basing your opinions on good trustworthy information? Is there even a chance that you are jumping to conclusions based on limited information?

Survey – Part 2

- I am going to ask three questions again. Let's see if there is any change in the result.

- Number one – put up your hands if you are *certain* that Christianity is boring. (Estimate the percentage of the group that have their hands in the air.)

- Number two – put up your hands if you are *sure* the claims of Christianity are untrue. (Estimate the percentage of the group that have their hands in the air.)

- Number three – put up your hands if you *know* Christianity is irrelevant to the life of a modern young person. (Estimate the percentage of the group that have their hands in the air.)

Note down the percentages again and comment if there is any significant change.

Conclusion

- If you think that there is even the smallest chance that you might have jumped to the wrong conclusion about Christianity (and might be making a mistake as big and potentially embarrassing as the Swiss estate agent) then why don't you check out the Youth Alpha course starting . . .

It's not boring, untrue or irrelevant to me.

Session 1 – Who Is Jesus?

Arrival – opener

Photocopy sheet 19. Images similar to *Hello* magazine or other 'celebrity' type publication. With the questions, 'Why are they famous?' 'How long will they be famous?'

Storytelling – in small groups

- Talk about the closest that you have come to fame. This might be your own moment of fame or a time when you came into contact with someone famous.

As this is the first session you should make sure that you start yourself, or else arrange with another confident member of the group to kick things off. Others will be happier about sharing their stories once one or two people have spoken.

Story presentation

The boat nosed towards the jetty and the crowd noise rose to a roar. Policemen in fluorescent yellow jackets linked arms and pushed back away from the shore, driving a wedge into the throng, forcing open a passage from the edge of the lake towards the narrow streets of the town. On the far side of the police line, a knot of press –photographers, reporters and cameramen – took up position at the land end of the jetty. Autograph hunters drove their elbows into the kidneys of those in front of them, followed elbows with shoulders and forced their way forward, fingering the shoot buttons of their Polaroid cameras. A couple of rough looking men leapt up off the boat and onto the jetty. They wore thick quilted jackets over roll-necked sweaters, and woollen hats pulled down to keep the cold sea wind off their heads.

In the first floor window of an expensive office building set just back from the lake, a pale man sat in a leather office chair. From his vantage point he could see the tight group still huddled down in the back of the boat, deep in conversation, it seemed. More men were up on the jetty now, looking angry and menacing – were they bodyguards, followers, or just hangers-on? Finally, the Master stood up; then bent to pull his two remaining companions to their feet. He balanced on the edge of the boat for a moment and then leapt into the arms of those on the jetty. The roar of the crowd, as they caught their first glimpse of the man they had come to see, carried above the howl of the wind. The pale man closed the window, carefully locked the door to his office and made his way downstairs.

Back behind the crowds, the pale man found a policewoman.
'Who's in charge here?' he asked.
The policewoman assessed him: well dressed, well spoken, but dishevelled – as if he'd been up all night. No alcohol on his breath, though. She hated these celebrity protection duties. How was she supposed to tell the crazies from the rest of the fans? She should be out catching criminals. Who'd want to stand all afternoon in the rain and the freezing wind just for a glimpse of today's joker? The stories about him were all lies; she would bet on it.
Finally, the policewoman answered, 'Inspector Stibbs. He's over there.' She waved vaguely in the direction of three police vans parked in a semicircle. Now the strange man was someone else's problem.
The Master walked on, his followers, more surly than ever, ringed him around like a hedge. They took no notice of the pale man in a suit, who stood off to one side, flanked by two police officers.

As they approached the man very carefully lowered himself down onto his knees. Looking up at the Master, his eyes suddenly filled with tears and he burst out, pleading with him.
'My daughter is dying. Master, come with me. Come and make her well. If you put your hands on her she will live.'

People quietened as news of the drama rippled through the crowd. The press hustled and soon the man was bathed in a pool of bright light that highlighted the expensive suit, now wet and dirtied from the pavement, and the look of anguish in his eyes.

'Come on then,' said the Master, holding out his hand to the man and hauling him to his feet. 'Let's see if we can't sort this out.'
(Based on Mark 5:21–24)

Responding to the story

- If Jesus were alive today, walking and talking, stalked by the paparazzi and hounded by the press, what would your attitude be?

- Which character do you think you are most like?
  Autograph hunter – just there for the experience and the boasting rights.
  Followers – 100 per cent committed to Jesus but perhaps not 100 per cent in tune with him.
  Press – a professional detached interest, they just want a story, real or fake.
  Policewoman – the sceptic, all that hype must be lies.
  Man – sees Jesus as the only person who can help him.

Go around the group and have each member pick the character that most closely resembles their approach to Jesus. If they are willing they should explain why they think this character fits them.

Teaching material

- People's approach to Jesus depends on who they think he is.

  - If you think he's a fake and a fraud then you can ignore him. If you think he is a wise teacher and philosopher then you can learn from his teaching, apply the bits that appeal to you and forget the rest.

  - Christians believe that Jesus Christ is the one and only Son of God – that he is both completely human and completely God.

  - Christians believe that he holds all of human destiny in his hands, that it is he who has the power to give and to take life, to judge and to forgive, to punish and reward.

  - If you believe this then it makes sense to worship him and live your life for him.

Bible reference: John 11:25–26

Discussion in small groups

- What do you make of the Christian claims?

- What sort of evidence would convince you to believe this?

- Could there possibly be any such evidence?

Closing

- In a moment of quiet we can all imagine what life would be like if the Christian claims were true.

- If Jesus were the Son of God how would it affect the way you live your life?

Why are they famous? How long will they be famous?

Session 2 – Why Did Jesus Die?

Arrival – opener

Photocopy sheet 20. Ladies, with the jewellery representing instruments of execution. With the question, 'Who is the odd one out?'

Storytelling – in small groups

- Tell of one incident in your life where you have had the chance to play the hero and save the day. For most of us, this could be quite commonplace like rescuing a cat from a small tree, or avoiding stepping on an ant, or it could be genuine heroism like saving somebody from drowning or. (If the group leader starts, ideally his/her story should be the least heroic of all.)

Story presentation

You might wonder what I'm doing here, in the jungle, walking, sweating and swatting flies. You might think I'm strange. If I tell you where I'm going you'll think I'm mad. I'm walking towards the guerrillas. Not gorillas – they're apes. I'm heading towards guerrillas – they're animals – responsible for kidnapping 3000 of my countrymen every year and for tens of thousands of deaths. I'm going to ask them to kidnap me, or at least take me in exchange for another of their prisoners.

So, you ask me why am I doing this? Why am I marching through the jungle, mile after mile, when I could be back at home watching MTV with the girls, or dancing with my boyfriend? I am doing it for Andres. I am going to see if the guerrillas will take me as their prisoner. Surely a sixteen year-old girl is a good hostage to have? 'Take me,' I will say. 'Take me and let that other man go.'

No, I've never met Andres. I first heard about him on the radio. Sometimes they slip in the news between the American songs that are my favourites. If you're fast you can change to another station, and keep the music flowing. But sometimes the news catches you. The story about Andres was interesting – or rather sad and terrible, I should say. All my friends were talking about

it at work and at school the next day. In the factory they turned the radio up extra loud every time the news came on, and at school even the teachers were discussing it. It was the kind of news that made you sad and angry at the same time.

Andres is 12-years-old. He has cancer. He is dying from it. He will die within weeks, perhaps before Christmas. The doctors in the hospital have already cut out a large part of his lung that had cancer in it, and now they've sent him home to his grandmother's house to die. There is nothing more that they can do for Andres, unless his father comes. If Andres' father comes, then perhaps he can donate a kidney to Andres, and perhaps Andres might live. But Andres' father isn't free to come. That is the problem.

And so I march. At first I took a bus. I caught it at the bus station in the centre of the city. I have travelled from there often with my mother and so I knew the way. I slept all night on the bus, only eating the biscuits I had brought with me, and once a pastry from an old woman who boarded the bus to sell food. She gave it to me cheap because she said I reminded her of her granddaughter. In the morning I had to get off the bus. The buses don't go close to guerrilla territory any more. Too many have been blown up by the guerrillas; too many passengers taken hostage and drivers killed. So I'm walking.

I'm walking because the guerrillas have Andres' father, Senor Perez. They have him and they won't give him back. They have had him for nearly two years, but they won't give him back in spite of everybody pleading with them. The President has asked them to give Senor Perez back. I went on a march with my brother and thousands of other students, 'Let him go!' we shouted, but the guerrillas didn't listen.

And so I'm marching. I am going to march right up to the guerrilla base – I know where it is – and I am going to make them release Senor Perez and let him go home to Andres. They can take me as a hostage in his place. Then, perhaps, Andres will live. At the very least he will have his father with him when he dies. And that will mean a lot. It would mean a lot to me.

- Based on the true story of the Colombian boy Andres Felipe Perez and of the teenager who marched through the southern jungle to the guerrilla safe-haven to offer an exchange. As reported in an article in the *Independent* newspaper, 4.12.01, p.14, by Jan McGirk.

Responding to the story

- How would you describe the teenager who marched up and offered herself to the guerrillas?

- Why do you think she did it?

- What is the most selfless thing anybody has ever done for you?

- Why do you think they did it?

Teaching material

- Christians believe that humanity has a problem. The wrongs that we have done, both collectively and as individuals, mean that death has entered the world, and after death, separation from God. Christians believe that Jesus came to earth to save humanity from their predicament. He died on the cross, but defeated death when he rose again, and so has the power to give us eternal life. He also destroyed the barrier that separated us from God. There are many, many ways to understand what Jesus did on the cross, each of them like the different facets of a beautiful diamond. What is

clear is that through Jesus we can have a relationship with God again.

Jesus' life and then death on the cross was the most heroic self-sacrifice in the history of the world. God became a man, he suffered and died to save us and draw us into relationship with him.

Bible reference: Romans 3:21–26

Discussion in small groups

- Would you agree that humanity has a problem?

- How would you describe this problem?

- Can you see how the death of Jesus on the cross can solve this problem?

- How would you feel if, as Christians believe, Jesus would have been willing to suffer all he did to save you alone?

- Do you think that eternal life is something positive?

- Do you think that relationship with God is something positive?

Closing

Play the song 'The Cross Has Said It All' by Matt Redman, or another that you are familiar with.

Photocopy Sheet 20 – Ladies with jewellery

Who is the odd one out?

Session 3 – How Can We Have Faith?

Arrival – opener

Photocopy sheet 21. An image of a bungee jumper throwing themselves out into nothing.
Comment 'Leap of faith'

Storytelling – in small groups

Tell of a time when you have had to make a 'leap of faith'. It might have been a bungee jump, or a climbing experience. It might simply have been choosing to trust a friend when you were doubtful. It can be a story of taking a leap of faith that came out well, or a leap of faith that turned out to be a mistake.

Story presentation

Jean-Francois Gravelet (1824–1897), better known as Blondin, was a famous tightrope walker and acrobat.

For Blondin the usual circus tricks were old-hat – there was barely any danger or excitement left in that as far as he was concerned. Not content with simply doing away with the safety net he went looking for new and more exotic challenges.

Eventually, he found somewhere to sling his tightrope that was guaranteed to thrill the crowds and bring sweat to the palms of everyone watching. He decided that he was going to make crossings of a tightrope 335 metres in length, suspended 50 metres above the Niagara Falls. Not surprisingly, large crowds, half terrified at the prospect of his falling and half wishing that the unthinkable would happen, watched his act.

Blondin liked to get the crowd really wound up. He began with a relatively simple crossing using a balancing pole. Then he would throw the pole away and begin a routine that truly amazed the onlookers.

On one occasion in 1860, a Royal party from Britain went to watch Blondin perform. He crossed the tightrope on stilts, then blindfolded. Next he stopped halfway to cook and eat an omelette. He then wheeled a wheelbarrow from one side to the other as the crowd cheered. He put a sack of potatoes into the wheelbarrow and wheeled that across. The crowd cheered louder. Then he approached the Royal party and asked the Duke of Newcastle, 'Do you believe that I could take a man across the tightrope in this wheelbarrow?'

'Yes, I do,' said the Duke.

'Hop in!' replied Blondin. The crowd fell silent, but the Duke of Newcastle would not accept Blondin's challenge.

'Is there anyone else here who believes I could do it?' asked Blondin.

Silence from the crowd. Seconds stretched into minutes and still no one answered Blondin's question. No one was willing to volunteer. Eventually, an old woman stepped out of the crowd and climbed into the wheelbarrow. To the delight of the crowd Blondin wheeled her all the way across and all the way back again.

The old woman was Blondin's mother. She was the only person willing to put her life in his hands.

Responding to the story

- Who do you identify with most? Are you an adventurer like Blondin or do you like to keep your feet firmly on the ground like the Duke of Newcastle?

- Can you imagine yourself taking up Blondin's challenge?

- What would persuade you to travel with him to the other side seated in a wheelbarrow?

  – Would you do it after watching him carry five other people across?

  – Would you do it if he promised you £1000?

  – Would you do it if your life was in danger and the crossing would save you?

- Why do you think Blondin's mother was willing to take the trip? Does this teach us anything about the nature of faith and trust?

Teaching material

Christianity recognises that to believe in God and to accept what Jesus has done for humanity requires a leap of faith. However, Christianity does not believe that this needs to be a leap in the dark. There are good reasons why we can be sure of our faith. The claims of Jesus and the New Testament of the Bible can be examined critically and intellectually. Many people have found themselves convinced when they started a study of this kind. There has not been time on this course but many Alpha courses take this approach.

There is a clue in the Blondin story. Blondin's mother was willing to take the leap of faith because she knew and loved her son. Christians believe that God is revealed in the Bible, particularly in the person of Jesus who was a perfect picture of God and said, 'If you have seen me you have seen the Father'. The God revealed in the Bible is completely loving and trustworthy. He will respond to our faith and not let us fall.
Bible reference: John 3:16

Discussion in small groups

- Does faith in God always have to be a 'leap in the dark' or are there reasons that we can be sure of our faith?

- Do you have any idea of how God is presented in the Bible?

- If so, do you think that the God pictured in the Bible inspires trust?

- What would it take to convince you to take a leap of faith and believe in God?

Closing

Have a moment of quiet. Invite people to close their eyes and then have someone read these verses about God from the Bible.

- 'Do you not know? Have you not heard? The Lord is the everlasting God, the Creator of the ends of the earth. He will not grow tired or weary, and his understanding no one can fathom.' Isaiah 40:28

- 'For the Lord is good and his love endures forever.' Psalm 100:5

- How priceless is your unfailing love! Both high and low find refuge in the shelter of your wings.' Psalm 36:7

- 'Can a mother forget the baby at her breast and have no compassion on the child that she has borne? Though she may forget, I will not forget you!' Isaiah 49:15

- 'For God so loved the world that he gave his one and only Son, that whoever believes in him shall not perish but have eternal life.' John 3:16

- 'But God demonstrates his own love for us in this: While we were still sinners Christ died for us.' Romans 5:8

- 'Whoever does not love does not know God, because God is love. This is how God showed his love among: He sent his one and only Son into the world that we might live through him.' 1 John 4:8–9

Leap of faith

Arrival – opener

Photocopy sheet 22.
Visual – two people obviously not communicating
Question, 'It's good to talk, isn't it?'

Storytelling – in small groups

- Talk of a time when you struggled to communicate. You might have been abroad, suffering from tonsillitis or in some other situation.

Story presentation

Ryan Faulkner's Story

I was brought up in Cape Town, South Africa. We were not a church-going family and the first time I ever went to church was at the age of 20. At school we had what was called a 'Bible education class' but it was more like a make-fun-of-the-teacher class.

After leaving school, I went to Cape Town University, where I studied Film and Television. I got involved in the party scene, going to clubs. I was into a lot of heavy music – heavy metal groups like Iron Maiden, Guns n' Roses, Megadeath, Metallica – and would go from wearing black clothes to the neon bright, screaming rave scene. It was pretty fun. As well as the raves, I was really into bikes – freestyle stuff, BMX-ing and motocross. I did a lot of freestyle motocross, where you hit jumps on your motorbike and you are 30 foot in the air and doing these tricks.

Then I applied for a two year working visa to the UK and thought, 'I'll go and have the biggest party in London.' I started off living in a backpacking hostel, but then I met a group of Kiwis, Aussies and South Africans and moved in with them. They would hold a party every night until three or four in the morning. There was a little bit of pot but nothing too serious. I found myself a job and it was pretty cool.

In the Autumn I got an e-mail from my mum in which she said she and dad had been on something called an Alpha course which they said was 'amazing'. As I read it I could sense a change in my mum, and my dad too. My dad would speak to me on the phone and say, 'I love you, son.' He had never said anything like that before.

All the time the e-mails from my mum and dad were saying things like, 'You have to do Alpha. But I thought, 'No, I'm just not for it.'

I had been going out with a girl in the house and we got really serious. But then she broke it off. Her visa was expiring and she was going back to South Africa. She broke the news to me in our bedroom and I couldn't handle it. I was so angry that I hit the door with my fist and broke it into little woodchips. My flatmates tried to intervene but in the end they called the police because they thought somebody was going to get hurt.

The cops came around and told me to leave for the night. They helped me pack a bag and before leaving I went and apologised to her, because I knew I would never see her again. As I left the house that night on the way to a friend's, I was walking to the tube station and I was feeling bad. I wouldn't say I was suicidal but I was really depressed.

As I walked, I thought of what my mum and dad had been saying and I said, 'If there is a God, show me. Prove yourself to me because I need help. You are meant to be this so-called wonderful God who can perform miracles. I need a miracle like pronto.'

There, sitting on a fence rail, was a tiny little wooden cross. I stopped and gently picked it up. Then I thought, 'Oh, this has to be some sort of sign. What are the chances of me just a couple of seconds ago asking God to show himself to me and then finding this.' I said to myself, 'I'm going to start an Alpha course.'

It was about Week 4 of the course that I really turned. When I got home, I said to God, 'Forgive me for everything I have done wrong. I want to turn over this new leaf and I want to start this new chapter in my life because clearly it's just amazing. I like what I see and I want what I see.'

Always before when I had wanted stuff it was all materialistic stuff like a helmet or a motocross kit. But this wasn't like that at all. I had to have a relationship with God and it was wild. Before, I thought of Jesus as just a swear word. We used to say that quite a lot. Now I feel very different about him. Now I appreciate that he died for the whole world.

Responding to the story

- Ryan's story could really be split into two halves, before and after his girlfriend dumped him. Which part of his story is most like your life? Do you relate to 'just having a party' or to 'searching for and finding God'?

- Ryan's parents became Christians on an Alpha course in South Africa. They changed and were keen to see him meet God too. Do you know of anyone who has become a Christian and then tried to persuade you to do the same? What do you think of that person?

- Ryan believed that God gave him a sign that he was real just when Ryan most needed it. Has God ever given you a sign? Or spoken to you in any way?

- By the end of the story it is clear that Ryan wants 'a relationship with God' more than he has ever wanted anything – and he gets it. Do you think 'a relationship with God' is something worth having?

Teaching material

Christians believe that 'a relationship with God' is the highest privilege a human can experience, and that it is a possibility for everyone – for all of us! In an earlier session we spoke of how Jesus' death on the cross destroyed the barrier that separated us from God, but the question now is, 'How can it be possible to have a relationship with someone you can't see or hear?'

Two key parts of the answer are prayer and the Bible. When Ryan said, 'If there is a God show me. Prove yourself,' he was praying. God answered his prayer by giving him the sign of the little discarded cross. Prayer is like having a hot-line to God. We can speak to him anytime and know that he hears us even if we don't get an immediate answer in the way Ryan did. The Bible is the main way that God speaks to us. It is his book, written by humans, but humans who were guided by God's Holy Spirit. Christians believe that with practice, over time, we can learn to hear God speak to us through the Bible.
Bible reference: Matthew 6:5–13

Discussion in small groups

- Have you ever tried praying? Did you have any indication that God might have heard you and even answered you?

- Do you think that it is possible to communicate with God through prayer?

- Have you ever tried to read the Bible? What did you think of it?

- Do you think that it is possible that God could speak to you through the Bible?

- Can you think of any other ways that God could speak to us as humans?

- Are you convinced that relationship with God is a possibility?

Closing

Allow a few moments of quiet at the end. Invite people that are still wondering if God is real, and whether a relationship with him is possible, to pray a simple prayer like Ryan's. They could invite God to make himself known to them.

Its good to talk, isn't it?

Session 5 – How Does God Guide us?

Arrival – opener

Photocopy sheet 23. Man in boat surrounded by vast expanse of water.

Comment, 'A little guidance would be nice'

Storytelling – in small groups

- Tell of the time in your life that you have been the most completely lost.

- You're here now, so what guided you back to safety?

Story presentation

Michael Bourdeaux is head of Keston College, a research unit devoted to helping Christians in what were communist lands. His work and research are respected by governments all over the world. He studied Russian at Oxford and his Russian teacher, Dr Zernov, sent him a letter which he had received because he thought it would interest him. It detailed how monks were being beaten up by the KGB and subjected to inhuman medical examinations; how they were being rounded up in lorries and dumped many hundreds of miles away. The letter was written very simply, with no adornment, and as he read it Michael Bourdeaux felt he was hearing the true voice of the persecuted church. The letter was signed Varavva and Pronina. In August 1964, Michael went on a trip to Moscow, and on his first evening there he met up with old friends who explained that the persecutions were getting worse; in particular the old church of St Peter and St Paul had been demolished. They suggested that he go and see it for himself.

So he took a taxi, arriving at dusk. When he came to the square where he had remembered a very beautiful church, he found nothing except a twelve-foot-high fence which hid the rubble where the church had been. Over the other side of the square, climbing the fence to try to see what was inside, were two women. He watched them, and when they finally left the square he followed them for a hundred yards and eventually caught them up. They asked, 'Who are you?' He replied, 'I am a foreigner. I have come to find out what is happening here in the Soviet Union.'

They took him back to the house of another woman who asked him why he had come. Whereupon he said he had received a letter from the Ukraine via Paris. When she asked who it was from, he replied, 'Varavva and Pronina'. There was silence. He wondered if he had said something wrong. There followed a flood of uncontrolled sobbing. The woman pointed and said, 'This is Varavva, and this is Pronina.'

The population of Russia is over 140 million. The Ukraine, from where the letter was written, is 1,300 kilometres from Moscow. Michael had flown from England six months after the letter had been written. They would not have met had either party arrived at the demolished church an hour earlier or an hour later. That was one of the ways God called Michael Bourdeaux to set up his life's work.

Responding to the story

- If you had to choose one of these words to describe the story above, which word would you choose: coincidence, luck, miracle, fate, destiny, guidance, chance.

- Have you ever experienced anything similar in your life? Would you use the same word to describe that experience?

- How do you think Michael Bourdeaux would explain what happened?

Teaching material

Christians believe that following God's plan is the way to live the best, most fulfilled, most exciting life possible. If that is true then it needs to be possible for God to guide us, to help us to make the right choices along the way and follow that plan. Being guided by God follows on naturally from having a relationship with God. God can guide us through the Bible, which has many general guidelines about how to live life; through the Holy Spirit, who can help us to hear God's voice; through common sense, God's given us brains and he expects us to use them; through advice from others, we all need help sometimes; and through circumstances, although not always so remarkably as in Michael Bourdeaux's experiences.

Bible reference: Jeremiah 29:11

Discussion in small groups

- How do you feel about God guiding you? How does the idea make you feel? Why?

- Do you think it is possible for God to guide you?

- If it is possible, on what sort of decisions, or on what occasions would you most value God's guidance?

- Have you ever felt that God was guiding you? Which of the methods listed above (Bible, Holy Spirit, common sense, advice, circumstances) did God use?

Closing

Take a few moments of quiet to think about a decision that awaits you in the near future. If you would like to, ask God to help to guide you to make the correct decision.

...a little guidance would be nice

Session 6 – How Can I Resist Evil?

Arrival – opening

Photocopy sheet 24. A spoof/fake horror film poster. Question, 'Evil, it's out there . . . but what is it?'

Storytelling – in small groups

- Invite the young people to talk about an experience in their lives under the title of 'My victory over evil.'

Story presentation

One bleak day the Sheriff of Nottingham, using trickery and deceit, cornered Little John and Robin Hood in a steep valley on the borders of Sherwood Forest. Robin and John were on horseback but unarmed. The Sheriff's men surrounded them and shot arrows into their horses, until the brave beasts fell to their knees, collapsed and died. Robin and John were incandescent with rage but the Sheriff wouldn't fight them.

'A quick death is too good for you,' he jeered. 'We're going to take you alive.' Eventually, when his forces outnumbered Robin and John by at least twenty to one, the Sheriff gave the order and sent his soldiers down the steep hillsides. They quickly overpowered Robin Hood and Little John.

Now that the Sheriff had his enemies in his power he accused them of horrible crimes that they hadn't committed. He called them murderers and traitors and had them dragged before a crooked judge. Then he imprisoned them in his deepest, darkest, dankest dungeon. When he wasn't too busy counting his money and cheating his peasants the Sheriff would descend the many flights of stairs to the dungeon to torture Robin Hood and Little John.

When the Sheriff had paid him enough money the judge officially found the outlaws, known as Robin Hood and Little John, guilty.
'Now you can have them hanged,' said the judge.
'Hanging is too good for them,' replied the Sheriff. 'I have slower methods.' The Sheriff prepared to execute them in his own way.

Maid Marion was beside herself with grief. Taking her life in her hands she went to the castle to beg the Sheriff for their release. A squad of heavily armed guards led her down the long stone corridors to the Sheriff's personal quarters. As he sat wrapped up in animal skins on his throne, Marion pleaded with the Sheriff for Robin and John's release. She made no secret of her love for Robin.

'I will give anything, do anything, if you will just let him out alive,' she said.
The Sheriff was a greedy man. He could never get enough money. And Robin was as good as dead anyway.
'Can you pay me?' he asked.
'I can't,' sobbed Marion. 'I have no money, and as a woman I own no property that I could will to you.'
Another idea struck the Sheriff.
'Would you sleep with me?' he leered. 'Do you love Robin that much? That's it! I'll only release your friends if you spend the night with me.'
With some considerable sadness, Marion at last agreed. The next morning, the Sheriff released his prisoners. Robin Hood and Little John were dragged up from the dungeon and staggered out of the castle. Blinded by daylight Robin fell into the arms of Marion who was waiting outside of the gate. She helped him to a cart and lay him on it, side by side with Little John. She drove them to the safety of the forest where she tended their wounds and nursed them to health.
Sitting around the campfire some nights later, Robin asked the inevitable question.
'Tell me how you did it,' he asked her. 'How did you persuade that vicious weasel to let us go? Did you trick him? Did the people give money to buy our freedom?'
Marion tried to hide the truth but she didn't have a story to satisfy Robin.
'Tell me what happened,' Robin demanded again, and now there was an edge to his voice.
Marion confessed. To her bewilderment and dismay Robin was outraged, he hurled abuse at her.
'Slut!' he shouted. 'I never want to see you again.'
When Robin drew back his hand to strike Marion, Little John intervened.
'No!' he said. Then he turned to Marion. 'Come with me. Let's leave Sherwood together. Ride away with me,

and I promise, you will have my life-long devotion.'
After a moment's silence and a long tortured look at
Robin, Marion accepted Little John's offer and they
rode away together.
(Adapted from Pip Wilson – *Stinking Magazine Book*)

Responding to the story

- Ask every individual in the group to make a list
  of the four principal characters in the story in the
  order of who is worst. The worst character is
  number one.

- Now take five minutes to work as a group to
  come to a consensus decision about the different
  lists you have made up.

Teaching material

It is not just the characters in the last story who act
badly, we all do, and in some ways it is the unjust
structures and distorted values of the world around us
that force us to act in the unpleasant ways we do.
Christians believe that directly or indirectly behind our
own evil desires and actions, and behind the
temptations, unjust structures and distorted values of
the world, lies evil personified – the Devil. It is the
existence of a personal devil that explains how a world
created by a good and loving God can contain evil
regimes, institutional torture and violence, mass
murders, brutal rapes, large scale drug trafficking,
terrorist atrocities, sexual and physical abuse of
children, occult activity and satanic rituals.

Christians do not believe in the Devil of old wives'
tales – with horns and a tail and a pitchfork. But they
do believe that the Bible, Christian tradition and
common sense all suggest the reality of an evil,
spiritual being who strives to destroy the world and its
human inhabitants whom God loves so greatly.

Fortunately, we do not have to fear the Devil. When
Jesus died on the cross and then rose again he inflicted
a terrible defeat on the Devil. Jesus has conquered the
Devil, and Jesus can therefore rescue us from the
Devil's influence. We can choose to live under Jesus'
rule where there is light instead of darkness,
forgiveness in place of guilt, love and not hate, life and
not death.
Bible reference: Colossians 1:13–14

Discussion in small groups

- Do you believe in the Devil? Why / why not?

- What do you think it means to say that Jesus
  'defeated' the Devil by dying on the cross and
  then rising again?
  Do you see any signs of this victory in the world
  around you?

- Do you find it reassuring to know that Jesus has
  won this victory?

- Is there anyone here who has had made the
  choice to live under Jesus' rule and not the
  Devil's?
  What difference has it made to your life?

Closing

Darken the room as far as possible. Then light a candle.

- Light always triumphs over darkness. Darkness
  can never overpower light.

Note: it is especially important to finish this session on
a positive note and not be too alarmist about the issues
discussed.

Evil, it's out there ... but what is it?

Session 7 – Telling Others and Healing

Arrival – opener
Photocopy sheet 25
A play on the whole contagion theme
Comment: 'Danger: highly contagious faith'

Storytelling – in small groups
- What is the best news that you have ever received?
- Who was the first person you told about it, and how did you tell them?

Story presentation
Ajay Gohill was born in Kenya but then came to England. He had been brought up as a Hindu and worked in his family business as a newsagent in Neasden. At the age of 21 he contracted erythrodermic psoriasis, a chronic skin disease. His weight dropped from 11.5 [73kg] to 7.5 stone [47.5kg]. He was treated all over the world – in the United States, Germany, Switzerland, Israel, and all over England including Harley Street. He said that he spent 80 per cent of his earnings on trying to find a cure. He took strong drugs which affected his liver. Eventually, he had to give up his job. The disease was all over his body from head to toe. He was so horrible to look at that he could not go swimming or even wear a T-shirt. He lost all his friends. His wife and son left him. He wanted to die. On 20 August he was in a wheelchair in the Elizabeth ward of St Thomas' Hospital. He spent over seven weeks in hospital receiving various kinds of treatments. On 14 October he was lying in his bed and wanted to die. He cried out, 'God if you are watching, let me die – I am sorry if I have done something wrong.' He looked in his locker and pulled out a Good News Bible. He opened it at random and read Psalm 38:

> O Lord, don't punish me in your anger! You have wounded me with your arrows; you have struck me down. Because of your anger, I am in great pain; my whole body is diseased because of my sins. I am drowning in the flood of my sins; they are a burden too heavy to bear. Because I have been foolish, my sores stink and rot. I am bowed down, I am crushed; I mourn all day long. I am burning with fever and I am near to death. I am worn out and utterly crushed; my heart is troubled and I groan with pain. O Lord, you know what I long for; you hear all my groans. My heart is pounding, my strength is gone, and my eyes have lost their brightness. My friends and neighbours will not come near me, because of my sores; even my family keeps away from me . . . Do not abandon me, O God; do not stay away from me, my God! Help me now, O Lord my saviour! (Psalm 38:1–11, 21–22 Good News Bible)

Each and every verse seemed relevant to him. He prayed for God to heal him and fell into a deep sleep. When he awoke the next morning 'everything looked new'. He went to the bathroom and relaxed in a bath. As he looked at the bathwater, he saw his skin had lifted off and was floating in the bath. He called the nurses in and told them that God was healing him. All his skin was new like a baby's. He had been totally healed. Since then he has been reunited with his son. He says that the inner healing that has taken place in his life is even greater than the physical healing. He says, 'Every day I live for Jesus. I am his servant today.' (Nicky Gumbel, *Alpha - Questions of Life*, Kingsway)

Responding to the story
- Can you believe that Ajay's story is a miracle; that God healed him? Why/why not?
- How does Ajay's good news – he was completely healed – compare with the good news stories the group talked about?
- Does it surprise you that Ajay considers his inner healing and his new relationship with Jesus as 'even greater' than his physical healing?

Teaching material
Christians believe that the best news that the world has ever received is the news that because of what Jesus has done humans can now have a relationship with

God. When this good news was first circulated by Jesus' disciples the excitement of the new faith became so contagious that Christianity spread around the Roman Empire and beyond in just a few years. Today, many Christians are a little more subdued about their faith, and aren't always so excited about sharing it with others. But Jesus commands Christians to share the good news with the people around them, especially those people that they care for.

One of the signs that the Christian faith truly is good news is healing. God healed Ajay to express the good news of his love for him, and after his healing Ajay entered into a new relationship with Jesus. Even today, when Christians share the good news God sometimes confirms his love and the truth of the Christian message by healing people.
Bible reference: Acts 3

Discussion in small groups

- Do you think of the Christian message as being good news?

- How good – lottery-win type good, or found-ten-pence-down-the-back-of-the-sofa type good?

- What do you think is the worst way of telling others about the Christian faith?

- What do you think is the best way of telling others about the Christian faith?

- Do you believe that God sometimes heals people as a means of making himself known to them? Why or why not?

Closing

- In a moment of quiet think about these two questions . . .

- Who is the person that you would most like to be able to give some fantastically good news to?

- How might you tell them the good news of the Christian faith?

DANGER: HIGHLY CONTAGIOUS FAITH

Session 8 – What about the Church?

Arrival – opener

Photocopy sheet 26

What image for the perfect example of interdependence, working together, teamwork, unity?

Storytelling – in small groups

- Ask each person to tell of his or her best or worst church experience. It could be a wedding, funeral, normal service, church parade, Christmas service – whatever.

Story presentation

The evening was not progressing as I had imagined in my daydreams. By the start of the gala I was a nervous wreck. In the half an hour before my race I was having to make frequent trips to the toilet. Five minutes before we were called, I looked so ill that people started asking me if I was going to be sick. Charlie was sitting beside me on the bench at the poolside.

'Don't worry,' he kept repeating over and over again. 'You'll do great. I know you will.'

'But the whole gala will be decided by these last two relays,' I moaned. 'What if I destroy our chances? No one will ever forgive me.'

'Dave, look at me,' said Charlie. I turned my head but even that much movement made me feel seasick. 'This is only a friendly gala; the result doesn't matter. It's just an overgrown practice. Now stop worrying.'

There wasn't much of an audience but all the teams sitting around the poolside were shouting and screaming as the last of the younger age group relays came to an end. In the enclosed and echoing swimming pool the noise was enough to make my head pound.

The tannoy crackled into life as the announcer called the competitors for my race. I was swimming the breaststroke leg of the senior medley relay, the penultimate race of the night. As the breaststroker I swam second, following Justin swimming backstroke. Then came Phil, swimming butterfly. Charlie would swim the anchor leg for us as he was the school's fastest front crawl swimmer.

We all gathered at one end of the pool to receive our instructions. Then, while Phil and Justin took their places at the starter's end of lane five, Charlie and I walked down the poolside to the far end of the lane. Just as we arrived the backstroke swimmers were called to enter the water and take their starting positions.

The silence terrified me, and as I stood alone on the edge of the pool I felt horribly exposed to the gaze of hundreds of pairs of eyes.

'Take your marks!' shouted the starter.

The only noise was the gentle lapping of the water beneath me. Time seemed to drag. My muscles tightened and I was sure everyone could see me shaking with fear and tension. Finally, the gun went off and Justin flung himself backwards in the water.

He got a good start, but as the eight swimmers moved down the pool towards me he seemed to be losing ground. He was in third place when Charlie started screaming at me to get ready. With my toes curled over the edge of the poolside I stood and shivered, tensed to dive the second Justin touched. Precisely as his hand collided with the end of the pool, I threw myself far out down the centre of the lane.

I fitted in my first stroke while still under water, then came up for breath. I could sense the swimmers on either side and ahead of me, but I refused to be distracted. Instead I focused on long, strong strokes, deep breaths and a fast rhythm. In what seemed like just a few seconds, I was near the end of the pool and needing to judge my line carefully so as to allow Phil room to dive in when I touched. I finished perfectly, just to the edge of the lane, and felt the backwash as Phil hit the water.

By the time I had climbed out and turned to watch, Charlie was on his way back towards me. With excitement I realised we were at least a metre ahead of the field. 'Phil must have swum a great length,' I thought. Then Charlie was home – in first place!

Before the slower teams had even finished, Charlie was shouting at the top of his voice, ignoring the stern looks of the lane judges.

'Dave, that was incredible,' he screamed. 'You gave Phil and me a two-metre head start.'
By then he was out of the pool, and by the time we had walked back to our team area the others had clustered around us. Sophie came up smiling, and her enthusiastic compliments made me grin like an idiot. We won the gala.
(Adapted from Jonathan Brant, *My Whole World Jumped*, Kingsway 2002)

Responding to the story

- Can you relate to Dave's experience

- Have you ever had a 'team' experience where everything came right? What happened?

- Do you think there is more pleasure in winning as a team or in winning as an individual?

Teaching material

Earlier people spoke of their worst experiences of church, and there is no doubt that church can be boring, strange and totally out of step with the life of a modern teenager. However, Christians believe that the church is actually something hugely important, beautiful and unique. For a start, the church is not a building; it is made up of people. Today's church is huge, at least 1,900,000,000 people, more than 34 per cent of the world's population. The church is all the people, Christians, who call God their Father. All members of the church are brothers and sisters as they have the same Father. God's goal is that the church should work together as a perfect team to show the rest of the world his love, and to bring the good news of the

Christian message to every person. In fact, the church is described in the Bible as more than just a team, as one body. Ideally, the different members of the church should work together as perfectly as the different parts of one body work together. To be a member of the church is to be a member of God's family, and a part of the largest team on earth, a team charged with the world's most important mission.
Bible reference: 1 Corinthians 12:1–26

Discussion in small groups

- Has what you have heard in this discussion changed the way you feel about the church? In what ways?

- Does it surprise you that there are so many Christians in the world today? (1,900,000,000)

- What would keep you from wanting to be a part of the church?

- What do you find attractive about the thought of being part of the church?

- Do you think that it is possible to be a Christian without being a part of the church?

Closing

- One of the keys to being part of a great team is being able to encourage one another. That is also one of the keys to being part of the church.

- As this is the final session of the course we are going to finish by going around the group and encouraging one another.

- As a group you must think of at least three encouraging things to say about each member. Think especially about their contribution to this course.

Photocopy Sheet 26 – On the dream team

SECTION VI
APPENDICES

Appendix I
Alpha Feedback Questionnaire

Name: _____

Group: _____

1. How did you hear about the Alpha course?

   _____

2. Why did you decide to do Alpha?

   _____

   _____

3. How many sessions did you attend?

   _____

4.a Were you a Christian when you started the course?

   _____

   Were you a regular churchgoer when you started the course?

   _____

b How would you describe yourself now (in terms of the Christian faith)?

   _____

c If the answer to a and b is different, when and how did the change occur?

   _____

   _____

   _____

   _____

   _____

5.   In what ways, if any, did you benefit from doing the Alpha course?

_____

_____

_____

_____

_____

6.   What did you enjoy most about Alpha?

_____

_____

_____

7.   What did you find most difficult?

_____

_____

8.   Which, if any, tapes did you buy? _____

9.   Which, if any, books did you buy? _____

10.   Did you find them helpful and if so why?
       (please name any books or tapes that you found particularly helpful)

_____

_____

11.   In what way could the course be improved?

a   Talks _____

_____

b   Small groups _____

_____

c   Generally _____

_____

12.   Any other comments

_____

_____

Appendix II
Sample parent release form

Name of parent(s)/guardian(s): _____

Contact telephone numbers (including mobile): _____

Contact telephone number if parent is not available: _____

Name of student: _____

Age: _____

Health information (especially allergies): _____

Dietary requirements: _____

I understand that my son/daughter will be in the care of the Alpha course leaders for the duration of the Alpha course.

Signed: _____   Date: _____

Appendix III
Registration Form

Please use this form to register your Alpha course if it is not already listed in *Alpha News*. The completed form should be returned in the envelope provided.

Registering your course is free of charge and enables us to list it in *Alpha News* and on our website. Information from the shaded boxes on this form will be placed on our website and given to anyone looking for a local Alpha course.

COURSE CONTACT

Title:

First name:

Surname:

Address:

County/Province:

Postal code:

Country:

Daytime telephone:

Home telephone:

Fax:

E-mail:

CHURCH LEADER

Title:

First name:

Surname:

Address:

County / Province:

Postal code:

Country:

Daytime telephone:

Home telephone:

Fax:

E-mail:

CHURCH/ORGANISATION DETAILS

Organisation name:

Denomination:

Mailing address:

County / Province:

Postal code:

Country:

Telephone:

Fax:

E-mail:

Website:

COURSE DETAILS

Course name:

Course denomination:

Course town (as you would prefer it listed in *Alpha News*):

Course County/Province: [   ]   Course postal code: [   ]

Country: [   ]

Date of first Alpha course at this church: [   ]   How many times has this church run Alpha? [   ]

Please tick type of Alpha course(s):   Daytime [   ]   How many people on your average daytime course? [   ]

Evening [   ]   How many people on your average evening course? [   ]

Youth [   ]   How many people on your average youth course? [   ]

How do you give the Alpha course talks?   Videos [   ]   Own speakers [   ]   Audio tapes [   ]   Combination [   ]

Data Protection Policy

The information you provide on this form will only be used for purposes directly connected with the Alpha Course. We never sell, rent or loan your personal information to others, although we sometimes pass your details to our Alpha Advisers and local conference organisers. We hold your details on computer under the terms of the Data Protection Act 1998.

[ ] If you would prefer your details not to be given to our trusted Alpha Advisers and local conference organisers for Alpha related activities only, please tick this box.

[ ] Please tick here if you don't want your name and daytime telephone number to be listed on our website search facility.

Appendix IV
Recommended Reading

Title	Author	Publishers	ISBN No.
Is There More to Life than This?			
Life, Death (and Everything in Between)	Mike Pilavachi & Craig Borlase	Hodder & Stoughton	0 3407 8592 6
Afterlife	Mike Pilavachi & Craig Borlase	Hodder & Stoughton	0 3407 3537 6
Why Jesus?	Nicky Gumbel	Alpha International	1 9040 7457 1
Who Is Jesus?			
Walking With a Stranger	Mike Pilavachi & Craig Borlase	Hodder & Stoughton	0 3407 3534 1
My Whole World Jumped	Jonathan Brant	Kingsway (2003 ed)	0 308 6172 X
Why Did Jesus Die?			
More Than Meets the Eye	Steve Chalke	Hodder & Stoughton	0 3406 4190 8
How Can We Have Faith?			
My First Trousers: Growing Up with God	Mike Pilavachi & Craig Borlase	Hodder & Stoughton	0 3407 3535 X
A Time to Jump	Malcolm Folley	HarperCollins	0 0027 4072 9
Soul Sista (For girls)	Beth Redman	Hodder & Stoughton	0 3407 5677 2
Street Children of Brazil	Sarah de Carvalho	Hodder & Stoughton	0 3406 4164 9
Run Baby Run	Nicky Cruz	Hodder & Stoughton (2003 ed)	0 3408 6196 7
Why And How Do I Pray			
For the Audience of One	Mike Pilavachi & Craig Borlase	Hodder & Stoughton	0 3407 2190 1
Why And How Should I Read The Bible?			
Downloading the Bible, Old Testament	Jonathan Brant	CWR	1 8534 5131 2
Downloading the Bible, New Testament	Jonathan Brant	CWR	1 8534 5132 0
YPs (Bible reading notes for 12–16 year olds)		CWR	
Holy Bible: New Living Translation		Tyndale House	0 8423 7576 7
Holy Bible: The NIV Youth Bible		Hodder & Stoughton	0 3406 5180 3
The Message: The Bible	Eugene Peterson	Navpress Publishing	1 5768 3289 9
How Does God Guide Us?			
Weeping Before an Empty Tomb	Mike Pilavachi & Craig Borlase	Hodder & Stoughton	0 3407 3536 8
Holy Spirit sessions			
Chasing the Dragon	Jackie Pullinger	Hodder & Stoughton (2006)	0 3409 0880 7
How Can I Resist Evil?			
The Screwtape Letters	C.S. Lewis	Fount	0 0062 8060 9
Why And How Should I Tell Others?			
Outwardly Active	David Westlake	Hodder & Stoughton	0 3407 8556 X
Mad for Jesus	Andy Hawthorne & Craig Borlase	Hodder & Stoughton	0 3407 4563 0
Does God Heal Today?			
Dancer Off Her Feet	Julie Sheldon	Hodder & Stoughton (2003)	0 3408 6158 4
What About The Church?			
What's So Amazing About Grace?	Philip Yancey	Zondervan	0 3102 4565 6
How Can I Make The Most Of The Rest Of My Life?			
Live the Life	Mike Pilavachi & Craig Borlase	Hodder & Stoughton	0 3409 0883 1
Jesus Freaks	DC Talk	Bethany House Publishing	0 7642 0084 4